YO-DIA-129

PHILIP II AND MACEDONIAN
IMPERIALISM

ASPECTS OF GREEK AND ROMAN LIFE

General Editor: H. H. Scullard

PHILIP II AND MACEDONIAN IMPERIALISM

J. R. Ellis

THAMES AND HUDSON

© 1976 THAMES AND HUDSON

All rights reserved. No part of this publication may be reproduced or transmitted in any form or by any means, electronic or mechanical, including photocopying, recording or any information storage and retrieval system, without permission in writing from the publisher. Not for sale in the United States of America, its dependencies, and the Philippine Republic.

PRINTED IN GREAT BRITAIN BY
COX & WYMAN LTD
LONDON, FAKENHAM AND READING

CONTENTS

PREFACE 6

CHRONOLOGY OF PHILIP'S REIGN 14

I MACEDONIA: PEOPLE, LANDSCAPE AND TRADITION 21

II THE ATHENIAN ALIGNMENT 45

III THE CHALKIDIAN ALIGNMENT 66

IV TOWARDS A GREEK SETTLEMENT 90

V THE UNEASY PEACE 125

VI BREAKDOWN 160

VII THE SECOND GREEK SETTLEMENT 181

VIII PHILIP, ALEXANDER AND PERSIA 211

APPENDIX 235

SELECT BIBLIOGRAPHY 240

NOTES 245

INDEX 309

PREFACE

TO A LARGE EXTENT THE RISE AND FALL of Philippic studies as well as the flux in attitudes towards Philip and his Macedonia have been governed by an inadequacy of sources – or at least of balanced sources. In broad terms the available evidence contemporary with the reign of Philip is not Macedonian but Greek; and at that mainly Athenian; and at that mainly anti-Macedonian. It is of course no absolute bar to the comprehension of any two opposing viewpoints that the one is expressed (even superlatively expressed) and the other distorted or altogether absent. Our almost total dependence on Tudor sources for the reign of Richard III has not prevented in recent times a more equitable study of the last Plantagenet. Julio-Claudian and late fifth-century Athenian studies have now begun to rise above the limits imposed by Tacitus and Thucydides respectively. The trouble with bias is not that it exists – not even that at times it may utterly dominate the evidence. What really matters is that it may go unrecognized; or, more often, improperly recognized.

There has recently been admirable illustration* of what is (or ought to be) a truism of historiography in general, that the development of Philippic studies over the past three centuries has been critically influenced – not to say determined – by the contemporary circumstances of the successive generations contributing to it. In the mid-nineteenth century, at a time of unparalleled social and political reform in his own country, for example, George Grote saw in the Greek city-state the sublimest expression of human individualism. To him, by consequence, Philip was the aggressor of the age, the 'destroyer of freedom and independence in the Hellenic world'. To the school of especially German historians who wrote in the aftermath of the successful unification movements of the later nineteenth century Philip appeared, on the contrary, to be the far-sighted unifier of a Hellenic motley (as the Englishman Hogarth saw him soon afterwards). The

* A. D. Momigliano, *Studies in Historiography* (London 1966) 56ff.

attitude of the historian has been the product to a significant degree of his own circumstances.

But that is inevitable. It is indeed the stuff of history, the exploration by a society of its own personal relationship with the past. (So each generation, as an act of selfconsciousness or as a means of fixing its identity, needs to rewrite it.) But in this particular case what is more serious is that, since all the sources are Greece- or Athens-oriented, the historian's viewpoint has been in practice the expression not so much of a relativity between himself and Philip as of his prior attitude towards the contemporary Greek world and, in particular, towards the Athenian *polis*. Thus, to those to whom the oratory of Demosthenes was the voice of freedom raised courageously against the dark forces of barbarian totalitarianism, Philip was – as one has said – no better than a Hitler, and Aischines his Quisling. To those whose political sensitivities were offended by the recalcitrant particularism of the Greek *polis*, by Demosthenes' fruitless attempts to resurrect those heroic days of a century earlier when Athens established her freedom to plunder and enslave the rest, Philip was a sort of prior-day Bismarck of the Hellenes.

While investigation of the impact of Philip on Athenian history is far from an unworthy occupation, it is as incomplete by itself as the study of the Persian Wars as an exclusive phenomenon of Greek history. The fourth century B C needs its Macedonian viewpoint. What the present work attempts to do, in a small way, is to evaluate Macedonia's own needs and interests, so far as they may be recovered, and the consequent internal constraints acting upon her domestic and especially foreign policies, with respect, at any rate, to the reign of Philip II.

It may be that the reader, like the author, will conjure to mind a picture of Philip the man. There will be those who are familiar with the small body of sayings attributed to him and with the little stories collected by much later authors purporting to reveal his character. It is my own view that these are by and large useless. Then there are such indications as contemporaries very occasionally give (Aischines, for example, on the king's charm towards the Athenian ambassadors in 346), which may, according to prejudice, be taken to disclose the real Philip – or no more than the political Philip. For Philip was, whatever else, a politician; and there are those who think of politicians as the little boy of popular myth thought of policemen, those he had always heard about and then those more benevolent gendarmes who bought him icecream to soften his judgement: there are the bastards and there are the cunning bastards. This book is not a biography. Such an exercise on the basis of such evidence is not possible. Thus it is not given the obvious title: Philip II of Macedon. For if it is naïve to speak of the causes of fourth-century Macedonian imperialism in terms of Philip's personal outlook (whether his supposed restless belligerence or, alternatively, some farsighted zeal for Hellenic unity), it must be the height of folly to do so on the basis of the sort of pseudo-evidence for it that survives.

And yet this has often been done. The remarkable explosion of social and military energy that propelled Macedon in hardly more than three decades from the periphery to the centre of eastern Mediterranean affairs has been put down to the private compulsions of one man. Certainly, the contributory and instrumental effects of Philip's early morale-boosting victories in 359 and 358 and his acquisition two years later of the rich Pangaian area beyond the Strymon have been given due weight. The necessary existing resources have not been overlooked, the large available manpower, the bounteous and secure food-supply and already better than modest reserves of copper and tin, gold and silver. But what is missing is the reagent, the factor or factors directly responsible for the massive forces now released for the first time. In the age of mass media the galvanic role of one man alone may be superficially credible, but hardly in a large and diverse ancient state.

If there had been in the past any single major reason for the impotence of Macedonia against its traditional predators – the Illyrians, Athens, Olynthos, even at times Thebes and Sparta – it had been the crippling absence of unity that was exploited time and time again by those with their own interests to serve. The primary manifestation of this disunity, admittedly shadowy even on the few occasions our sources allow some light to penetrate the curtain of obscurity, was the antagonism between Upper and Lower Macedonia, west and east.

But in Philip's reign, as the curtain lifts a little, a change takes place. Mostly dimly, but perceptibly, through such agencies as the transplantation of population-groups, the large-scale dilution of the noble *hetairos* class and the institution of the Royal Pages, a single nation takes shape. Even clearer in this process is the role of the army, probably in any case the only Macedonian institution capable of a pervasive and comprehensive national role. Through the subordination of the regionally recruited *taxis* to the nationally organized militia, by the provision of attractive monetary and status inducements to loyal service in the national body, by the making feasible continuity of service in it by grants of land at least to the officers and probably to their men, and particularly by the laying of a heavy emphasis on an institution whose natural orientation was towards its apex rather than its extremities, there grew during this reign an allegiance to the single nation, through its army, and to the king-commander as the single head.

There can be little doubt as to the centrality of Philip's part in the process. While the vital elements were already there the realization of their potential was his achievement. But if the army was at once the instrument and the expression of the new unity it was all the more essential that military objectives were constantly in mind and, more important, that military successes were won, lest it turn the newly found energies in upon itself and the state. While, that is, the revolution was at least shaped by Philip's own determination and perception, he was as bound as anyone else by its implications; he was the rider of the tiger he had released.

This is not to say, however, that Philip can have occupied the Macedonian throne in 359 already convinced that military expansion would provide all or indeed any of the answers to his difficulties. In the context of the first years of his reign, when to survive must have been ambition enough, expansionary imperialistic aims were the indulgent fantasies of a dreamer. But here again we have suffered at the hands of our sources. Our most impressive contemporary author, Demosthenes, does not touch on Philip until the end of the 350s (although Demosthenes' Athens had already been formally at war with him for several years), by which time Macedonia was becoming a power to be reckoned with, and he judges this king's early reign in the light of the achievements of later years. The same is true of other sources. These northern fringe-dwellers of the Hellenic world were simply not noticed by literate contemporaries until Philip's successes compelled their attention; and, when they did notice, they naturally saw in the previous years an inevitable and, worse, calculated rise to that level of prominence and influence. But when Demosthenes, in a speech on another subject in 351 (*On the Rhodians* 24), implicitly chides his fellow Athenians with dismissing Philip as a person of no account, we should not miss the obvious: that that, even yet, was how he could be seen.

In 359, with a multitude of dangers pressing upon him and his factious kingdom, Philip had, among other things, to face a question that had constantly exercised his predecessors: where would he find a protective alliance reliable enough to allow him reasonable security in the Aegean context while he endeavoured to ease the pressures from his immediate neighbours and within Macedonia? At that time, in fact, the choice was not difficult. Athens appeared currently within reach of the power she had exercised over her fifth-century alliance. In the late 360s, as the ineffectual sanctions of the Persian king's Common Peaces were increasingly recognized as the mere bluff of the preoccupied, and as the last remnants of Spartan power fast dissipated, Athenian ambitions in the Aegean (like those of Thebes by land) had become more and more transparent. Philip sought refuge under the expansive umbrella of Athenian power.

But little more than two years later the Athenian alliance was torn apart by the revolt and secession of some of its wealthiest and most powerful members. Here the king faced a second critical decision. He was in no position to assist his embattled ally, not least because he himself had no navy, so he might either chance his fortunes utterly on the strength and determination of Athens or cast himself loose in search of another support. His choice was the correct one; in 355 the Athenians were to accept the ultimatum of the Persian Artaxerxes Memnon and, humiliated and exhausted, surrender their claims on the growing naval alliance. Absolved of the need, by the end of 357, to subordinate his own interests to those of his ex-ally, Philip took Amphipolis. With Athens' own problems absorbing all of her energy and resources, he need fear no immediate consequences. By ceding the rich Anthemous valley and assisting in the suppression of Poteidaia – the magnitude of the concessions neatly underscoring the weakness from which Macedonia bargained – he won the alliance of the Olynthians and, with the reassuring presence of a friendly Chalkidian League at his Aegean side, was able to continue the tasks of building his army, reorganizing his state and strengthening its frontiers.

From 356 Macedonian influence began to spread beyond the frontiers, in Thrace and Thessaly. From his involvements during these years it becomes clear from what directions the king expected danger would come, for, whereas on the western, northern and northeastern sides little more was done than to launch the occasional punitive or pre-emptive strike, to the east and south, on the other hand, he devoted considerable time and care to the establishment of firm relations and reliable governments. Along the Aegean coastline of Thrace, moreover, he systematically picked off the maritime towns that might serve as bases for any resurgent Athenian naval power. But in 353 defeat came close to expunging all his achievements. In the shock wave that passed through his allied and buffer states following a serious loss in Thessaly, influence in eastern Thrace passed to Athens, to whom the Olynthians too began making overtures of peace, and in several other areas the Macedonian links were dislocated. Some of the damage was repaired quite quickly, thanks mainly to the remarkable success of Philip's Thessalian campaign of 352. But the strains in the Macedonian relationship with Olynthos remained to be repaired and its interests in eastern Thrace to be recovered.

However, although the kingdom could even yet offer no overwhelming challenge to the major Greek states, the Thessalian triumph of summer 352 might be seen as a portent – welcome to some, chilling to others. Most importantly, Philip's successes had brought him to the point where he stood on the threshold of central and southern Greek affairs, affairs which must concern him vitally as they had some of his predecessors, and affairs over which he need not even take any initiative to become involved, for he already had allies (including the Thessalian League and, by this time, perhaps Thebes) who would relish his participation in the debilitating Sacred War in Central Greece. It is at this point that his third critical decision had to be made; and, to understand it, we need to keep in mind the internal socio-military pressures in Macedonia, which by now must have been a factor impressing itself on the king's attention, and to apply some hindsight.

In 338/7, after the conclusion of Common Peace among the Greek mainland states (the so-called League of Korinth), Philip proclaimed his intention to lead eastwards a crusade that would enlist the Hellenes as his allies. He withdrew then from Greece and never saw it again; and neither, probably, would his son Alexander have returned there had dissensions not broken out on his father's assassination. The League of Korinth, that is, marked the end of the deliberate extension of Macedonian influence in the Greek peninsula. But a careful examination of the king's purpose in negotiating with Athens the Peace of Philokrates eight years before that time indicates that what he achieved in 338/7 had also been his intention in 346. It was this purpose – to make Greece safe for his own withdrawal for the greener pastures of Anatolia – that he must have determined upon at the end of the 350s or very early in the 340s. In its execution Hellas was to be a source of co-operation, assistance, even inspiration (and, above all, he must be certain that it would not erupt in his rear), but it was not in that direction that he sought to give rein to the military energies of his own society. When it came to the search for longer-term and profitable military objectives it was to the barbarians of Asia Minor that he turned.

Thus, around 350 as the Chalkidian alliance slipped away from him, he laid his plans for the master-stroke that would follow the now expedient obliteration of Olynthian power. The most potent coalition he must fear among the Greek states was that of Athens and Thebes. In the immediate future it was not a likely event, but the one way to ensure that the hoplite army of Thebes, its strength so convincingly demonstrated (to the cost, among others, of Macedonia) during the 370s and 360s, would never be used against him was to strip from the Thebans the foundation of their power, the Boiotian and other neighbouring areas under their domination. To balance and control a weakened Thebes he would make use of Athens, upon whose co-operation he would depend. To this end he designed the Peace of Philokrates. Under its regulation would be established, in effect, a co-hegemony over the Greek world, with the Athenians again free to control the seas and able, at least with Macedonian support, to maintain peace among the Hellenes. Access to her Black Sea grain sources would be guaranteed Athens by her ally's control of Thrace. As Philip's military needs drew him towards Asia Minor, Athens' navy would render assistance and stand ready to open its economic resources to Aegean trade. Fundamentally, of course, the partnership would be unequal; but against this the Athenians would be able to balance the rewards accruing to them.

In many ways such an arrangement had been foreshadowed not long before in the relationship between Persia and Sparta in the Common Peaces of 387/6 and the 370s. In these, in effect, the one power stood as guarantor, the other as executor of a hegemonial structure imposed upon the Hellenic states. But where the Common Peaces had broken down – in the failure of Persia to prevent the growth of Athenian naval and Theban land power and in the inability of the depleted Spartan population and its reactionary army to match the Theban hoplite on the battlefield – the Peace of Philokrates might have stood firm, based on what would be the strongest army and what was already the strongest navy of the Hellenic peninsula.

Such a settlement of Greek affairs was not to be. Nearly a decade was lost as Philip struggled at first to save and then to replace a peace aborted just before birth. Its substitute, the League of Korinth, was in at least one sense the inferior of the ill-starred predecessor, in that its realization had to follow a war whose fears and hatreds must blunt the possibilities of willing association among recent adversaries. But its effect was much the same – or would have been had its architect and engineer not been struck down soon afterwards by the assassin's dagger.

It is thus the general conclusion of this study that Philip (as much as Alexander after him) was no solitary phenomenon of Macedonian or Greek history, materializing from nowhere without impetus, explanation or context. Philip did contribute much of his own to the shaping of what can only be thought of as a major social and military revolution, initially by his skilful organization of the necessary means of survival and later by his recognition and exploitation of the forces he had released in doing so; and to this positive and dominant theme the debility of a Greek world racked for many decades by war and dissension played a matching counterpoint. But the expansive force itself, perhaps largely the product of a newfound security and confidence, came to exist in a sense separately from the king and to govern his actions and policies. To say only this, however, is to suggest that Macedonian imperialism was undiscriminating and undirected, which, as this work attempts to show, is not the case. The course set by Philip may have gone unrecognized by some of his contemporaries, but not by all, and it is still indentifiable; and that, by means of a progressive investigation of the whole reign, is the major purpose here.

The spelling of Greek names has presented no less than its usual difficulty and has been tackled with no fewer than the usual inconsistencies. There is no particularly good reason in the twentieth century for Latinizing a Greek name and I have not done so where it was comfortably avoidable. As to Anglicized or the especially common Latin forms, the worst to be said of them is that they lend a spurious familiarity to what ought to be exotic and alien. A rough Upper Macedonian tribesman should sound more credible as Alexandros (better still with the Modern Greek stress accent on the second syllable) than as friendly, suburban Alexander. But since gentlemen of that name abounded I found it convenient to refer to the Alexanders of the Argead family while leaving their foreign and country namesakes unblemished. Otherwise, with Macedonian people and places (with the single exceptions of the kingdom itself and its king), the Greek form is retained. With other names the same convention is observed (*e.g.* Delphoi and Aischines), other than in cases of the very familiar (Aristotle and Athens) or the otherwise disagreeable to eye or ear (Cyprus, Thucydides and Thrace).

The extent of my heavy indebtedness to the scholarship of others I hope I have been able to make clear in my notes, appendix and bibliography. What I owe to the encouragement and advice of friends and colleagues is more difficult to record – not for lack of gratitude but for fear of omission; but I can not pass this opportunity of expressing my appreciation of help received at one time or another from Professors C. F. Edson, N. G. L. Hammond, M. M. Markle, R. D. Milns, G. le Rider and P. R. C. Weaver. My work has been materially assisted by the generosity of the Institute for Balkan Studies in Thessaloniki, the Myer Foundation together with the Australian Humanities Research Council and, especially, Monash University. To the British School of Archaeology at Athens, a convenient base for travel and an ideal milieu for reading and conversation, I owe several pleasant and fruitful months.

Monash University J.R.E.
Victoria, Australia
1975

THE CHRONOLOGY OF PHILIP'S REIGN

Abbreviations
c. = *circa*;   e. = early;   m. = middle;   l. = late
W = Winter   Sp = Spring   S = Summer   A = Autumn
i   = January,   ii = February,   iii = March, etc.

ATTIC MONTHS:
  I = Hekatombaion   VII = Gamelion
  II = Metageitnion   VIII = Anthesterion
  III = Boedromion   IX = Elaphebolion
  IV = Pyanepsion   X = Mounychion
  V = Maimakterion   XI = Thargelion
  VI = Poseideon   XII = Skirophorion

Note: in theory, i (January) coincides with the Attic month VII (Gamelion), ii (February) with VIII (Anthesterion), *etc.*, but in practice, since the Attic year lasted 354 days (in twelve months of 29 and 30 days alternately), the needs of periodic intercalation (when it was done properly: three 'full' months – i.e., of 30 days each – during each eight-year cycle) mean that coincidence between the two calendars can never be taken for granted. Thus, when Attic dates are known, I have given them; otherwise Julian months, seasons, years represent declining orders of chronological precision.

359   (W) Philip's accession.
      Treaty with Bardylis; Philip marries Audata.
      Macedonian troops withdrawn from Amphipolis.
      Philip contacts Kotys of Thrace; Pausanias is killed.
      Argaios at Methone; marches to Aigai; is defeated by Philip.
      Peace with Athens.
      (A ?) The Paionians are suppressed.

358   (Sp?) Bardylis & his Dardanians are defeated.
      Upper Macedonia annexed.
      Philip aids Aleuadai of Larisa; he marries Philinna.

357 (S) Athens recaptures Euboia from Thebes.
Macedonian alliance with Epeiros; Philip marries Olympias.
Athens forms alliance with the three Thracian kings.
(e.W) Outbreak of Athens' Social War.
(W) Philip takes Amphipolis; Athens declares war.

356 Philip takes Pydna.
(Sp) Macedonian/Chalkidian alliance.
Appeal from Krenides.
Theban attack on Phokis & Sparta in Amphiktyonic Council.
(S) Foundation of Philippoi.
Coalition: Ketriporis, Lyppeios & Grabos against Macedonia.
The Phokians seize Delphoi.
(I) Athens joins the northern anti-Macedonian coalition.
The birth of Alexander.
The northern coalition (minus Athens) is defeated.
Capture of Poteidaia, which Philip hands to Chalkidians.
Capture of Apollonia, Galepsos & Oisyme (or e. 355?).
Phokian alliances with Athens, Sparta & other Peloponnesians.

355 (Sp?) Philip again lends troops to Larisa to resist Pherai (?).
(X/XI) Neapolis appeals to Athens.
(m.S) Athens' Social War ends; her alliance crumbles.
(A) The Amphiktyony declares sacred war on Phokis.
(W) Philip invests Methone.

354 (Sp) The Phokian Philomelos takes the offensive in Central Greece.
Methone falls to Philip; he takes Pagai.
(S/A) He moves along Thracian coast, takes Abdera & Maroneia.
Philip/Kersebleptes agreement.
Chares attempts to ambush Philip's small fleet at Neapolis.
Thessalian request for further aid.
Philomelos falls at Neon; Onomarchos takes the Phokian command.

353 (Sp) Onomarchos convenes the rebel Amphiktyony; he campaigns successfully (in Sp & S) in Western Lokris, Doris, Boiotia & near Thermopylai, but is defeated near Chaironeia.
Chares captures Sestos & campaigns against Kersebleptes.
(S) Philip enters Thessaly & drives back Pheraian/Phokian allies.
(A) Onomarchos advances into Thessaly; the Allies defeat Philip & the Thessalians; Philip withdraws to Macedonia.
Kersebleptes accepts Chares' terms; alliance with Athens.
Athens sends cleruchs to the Chersonesos.
Olynthos declares friendship for Athens & requests alliance.

Artabazos & Memnon granted refuge at Pella.

352 (l.W) Onomarchos campaigns in Boiotia, takes Koroneia (& Korsiai & Tilphosaion?).
(Sp) Philip returns to Thessaly, is elected Archon of the Koinon (or S 353?).
Onomarchos marches towards Pherai; Chares sails for Pagasai.
(Sp/S) Philip takes Pagasai & defeats Phokians on Krokion Plain.
Pherai surrenders; Philip expels tyrants & marries Nikesipolis.
Cession to Philip of Pagasai & parts of Perrhaibia & Magnesia; Macedonian colony founded at Gonnoi.
(m.S) Philip advances to Thermopylai, finds it defended, withdraws.
(V) Philip reaches Heraion; alliance with Byzantion, Perinthos & Amadokos against Kersebleptes.

351 (Sp) Last meeting of rebel Amphiktyony.
Boiotian & Phokian troops in Peloponnesian War.
(I/II) Philip falls ill in Thrace.
(III) The Thracian campaign ends.
Philip's warning to the Chalkidians.

350 Campaigns in Paionia & Illyria?
Campaign in Epeiros; Arybbas becomes regent; Alexandros to Pella.

349 (S ?) Return of tyrants to Pherai.
(c. ix) Invasion of Chalkidike begins; Philip takes Stageira. (A) Demosthenes delivers Olynthos; Olynthian/Athenian alliance.
Philip expels Pheraian tyrants again.

348 (VIII-IX) Athenian intervention in Euboia.
(Sp) Philip resumes Chalkidian campaign.
(S ?) Aristotle leaves Athens.
(vi) Euboians bring news of Philip's friendship to Athens.
Philip invests Olynthos itself.
Capture of Phrynon of Rhamnous.
Ktesiphon sent to Philip.
(viii/ix) Fall of Olynthos.
Ktesiphon brings Philip's good will; Philokrates proposes peace-talks, & is prosecuted, defended by Demosthenes & acquitted.
(W) Euboulos' decree (Aischines goes to Arkadia).

347 (Sp/e.S) Phalaikos removed from Phokian command.
(I) Demosthenes & Philokrates enter Boulē.
Athens co-operates with Kersebleptes in setting up Thracian coastal fortresses.

(l.S) Philip intervenes half-heartedly in C. Greece.
(W) Siege of Halos begins.
Phokian triumvirate offers Thermopylai to Athens & Sparta.

346 (i) Athenian decree inviting Hellenes to join in war or peace.
(VII) Phalaikos recovers Phokian command.
(e. VIII) Iatrokles returns; Aristodemos reports; Proxenos' letter arrives; Embassy I leaves for Pella.
(m. VIII) Embassy I arrives in Pella.
(*c*.20. VIII) Embassy I leaves for home; Philip leaves for Thrace.
(*c*.27. VIII) Embassy I arrives home; reports to Boulē & Assembly.
(9–13. IX) City Dionysia (during which Macedonian envoys arrive?).
(18/19. IX) Athenian Assemblies vote for peace & alliance, but excise exclusion-clause from Philokrates' decree.
(23. IX) Surrender of Kersebleptes to Philip.
(24. IX) Athenians & their synod-members give oaths to Macedonian envoys; exclusion-clause reinstated *de facto*.
(3. X) Embassy II leaves Athens.
(*c*.26. X) Embassy II arrives in Pella.
(*c*.22. XI) Philip returns home to meet Athenian & other embassies.
(13. XII) Macedonians in Thermopylai; Embassy II arrives home.
(16. XII) Assembly confirms & extends alliance; promises aid.
(*c*.17. XII) Embassy III leaves for Thermopylai *via* Euboia.
Demosthenes & Timarchos impeach Aischines.
(*c*.18. XII) Philip despatches letter(s) requesting Athenian aid.
(*c*.20. XII) Assembly considers & rejects the request.
(23.XII) The convention between Philip & the Phokians.
(25. XII) Embassy III at Chalkis hears the news & turns for home.
(27. XII) Embassy III reports to Assembly at Peiraieus.
(I) Special Amphiktyonic Assembly at Thermopylai.
Athenian prisoners released by Philip.
(II) The Pythia held with Philip presiding; Athens abstains.
(III) Amphiktyons demand Athenian assent to recent decisions; Demosthenes: *On the Peace*; Athens backs down.
(IV) Autumn Pylaia.
(W – 346/5) Aischines successfully counter-impeaches Timarchos. Antiphon tortured & executed.

345 (Sp) Amphiktyons support Athens over control of Delos.
Philip reorganizes population-groups.
He campaigns against Illyrian Pleuratos.
Isokrates: *epistle* 2.
(A) Megalopolis & Messene (*et al.*?) admitted to Amphiktyony.

344 (S) Philip enters Thessaly, puts down revolts, garrisons Pherai under dekadarchy, reintroduces tetrarchic national government. Demosthenes goes to Peloponnesos as envoy.
(m/l. S) Philip sends Python to Athens; Demosthenes' *Philippic* II. Athens rebuffs Persian embassy.
(A/W) Hegesippos in Pella.

343 (Sp) Thebans press for Phokian reparations to begin.
(S) Philokrates impeached, flees.
Stasis in Elis & Megara.
Philip refuses aid for Kallias of Chalkis.
Pro-Macedonian factions dominant in Eretria & Oreos.
(A) Trial of Aischines.
Phokian reparations begin.
(A/W) Philip sends final offer of Common Peace to Athens & himself goes to Epeiros.

342 (W) Philip removes Arybbas, installs Alexandros on Epeirote throne; he adds Kassopeia to Molossian Koinon.
Athens sends troops to Akarnania & envoys seeking alliances in western Greece & the Peloponnesos.
(l.S) Aristotle goes to Pella & then Mieze as Alexander's tutor.
(vi) The final campaign in Thrace begins.
(S/A) Hipponikos, Eurylochos & Parmenion in Euboia periodically.
Philip consolidates Macedonian hold on south coast of Thrace, forms alliance with Getai in the north; he marries Meda.
(A) Antipatros presides at the Pythia.
(W 342/1) Violence between Kardia & Athenian cleruchs in the Chersonesos.
Establishment of military colonies in Hebros Valley.
Macedonian herald (Nikias) kidnapped by Athens.

341 (Sp) Philip sends troops to Kardia; calls for reinforcements.
Diopeithes attacks Thracian towns.
Philip sends envoy, whom Diopeithes tortures & ransoms.
(Sp) Athens/Chalkis alliance.
(l. Sp) Demosthenes: *On the Chersonesos*.
(e.S) Hermias kidnapped, tortured & killed.
Demosthenes: *Philippics* III & IV.
(S) Philip defeats Teres & Kersebleptes, removes them from thrones.
(S/A) Oreos & Eretria taken by Athens.
(A) Demosthenes, Hypereides, etc., as envoys to Byzantion, Perinthos, Selymbria, Chios, Rhodos & Persia.

Philip campaigns on west coast of Black Sea.
(W 341/0) Demosthenes & Kallias canvass support in W. Greece & the Peloponnesos.

340 (l.W) Demosthenes & Kallias report great successes & hoodwink the Athenian *demos* into approving Euboian League under Chalkis.
(Sp) Philip attacks Perinthos.
Phokian reparations halved.
(m.S) Philip's letter ([Dem.] XII); the Macedonian fleet is escorted into the Propontis; Persian opposition.
(e.A) Philip invests Selymbria, advances to Byzantion.
He captures the corn-fleet.
(ix/x) Athens declares war.
Alexander defeats the Maidoi & founds Alexandropolis.
Chares bottles up Philip's fleet in the Black Sea.
(l.A/e.W) Phokion replaces Chares at the Propontis.
(?) Philip sends aid to the Skythian Ateas, but is rebuffed.

339 (l.W) Philip makes peace-overtures towards Byzantion, etc.
Tricking Phokion, he extricates his fleet.
(Sp/S) The Skythian campaign.
(Sp) Amphiktyonic charge of Amphissian sacrilege.
(v/vi) Amphiktyonic meeting at Thermopylai; campaign against Amphissa.
Thebes seizes Nikaia.
(S) The Macedonian army, after Triballian defeat, returns home.
(A) Sacred War declared against Amphissa; Philip elected Hegemon.
(x/xi) Philip occupies Kytinion & Elateia.
(xi) Macedonian & Athenian envoys at Thebes.
Theban/Athenian alliance; defence-forces in Gravia Pass & at Parapotamioi.
(W 339/8) Philip beaten back in two skirmishes near Kephisos.

338 (Sp) Philip tricks defence-forces in Gravia Pass; Parmenion captures Amphissa, moves to Delphoi, takes Naupaktos & hands it to Aitolians.
Athens, Thebes *et al.* fall back to Chaironeia.
(7.II) Battle of Chaironeia.
Athenian settlement.
Theban settlement.
Further settlements in Central Greece.
Isokrates' *epistle* 3.
(x/xi/xii) Settlements in the Peloponnesos.
Delegates called to Korinth; proposal of Common Peace.

337 (W/Sp) Second meeting at Korinth; Common Peace established; sacred war declared against Persia.
(Sp/S) Philip returns to Macedonia; he marries Kleopatra.
Exile (?) of Alexander & Olympias; both soon recalled.
Campaign against Illyrian Pleurias.
Marriages of Attalos to Parmenion's daughter & Amyntas to Kynnane.
Pixodaros affair (or Sp. 336)

336 (Sp) Advance-party under Parmenion crosses to Asia Minor; the Greek cities & islands begin to join the Common Peace.
(S) Marriage of Alexandros of Epeiros to Philip's daughter Kleopatra; the assassination of Philip.

CHAPTER I

MACEDONIA: PEOPLE, LANDSCAPE AND TRADITION

ONE IS HARD PRESSED TO COMPREHEND the lasting forces that shaped the character of the ancient Greek and his polis without a firm appreciation of the geographical and topographical features of his peninsula, features that more perhaps than anything else have borne the responsibility for the comparative continuity of Hellenic society through the ages in the face of immigrations, occupations, political dismemberment and arbitrary reconstruction. But not much less fundamental to the historical processes played out upon this peninsula are the very different characteristics of the southern Balkan region, whence it protrudes into the Mediterranean basin. If the predominating feature in the formation of the peninsular societies was the mountain-ranges that separated and circumscribed them in small inland and coastal spaces, that limited their agrarian capacities and forced many to turn their eyes to the sea for trade and communication, in Macedonia – though the mountains are there too – it was more the extensive, fertile plains carrying large populations of more loosely knit tribal organizations that shaped these frontier-people of the Greek world. The society nurtured on these plains was quite different from those of the bulk of the contemporary Hellenic world, in the fourth century BC still more akin in many ways to the heroic kingdoms of Homeric times.

KINGS AND KINGSHIP

For formal purposes the king himself was the state; in documents of state his name alone, ungarnished by title and uncomplemented by other executives, stood for Macedonia.[1] (Where the title – King of the Macedonians – was included, which is extremely rare at this period, it seems to have been only when the king was to be represented or addressed as an individual and not as the state.)[2] For example, in the Delphic hieromnemon-lists, by contrast with the delegates of all other Amphiktyonic tribes, whose representation was expressed in the form of ethnics, the Macedonians were styled simply 'those from Philip' or

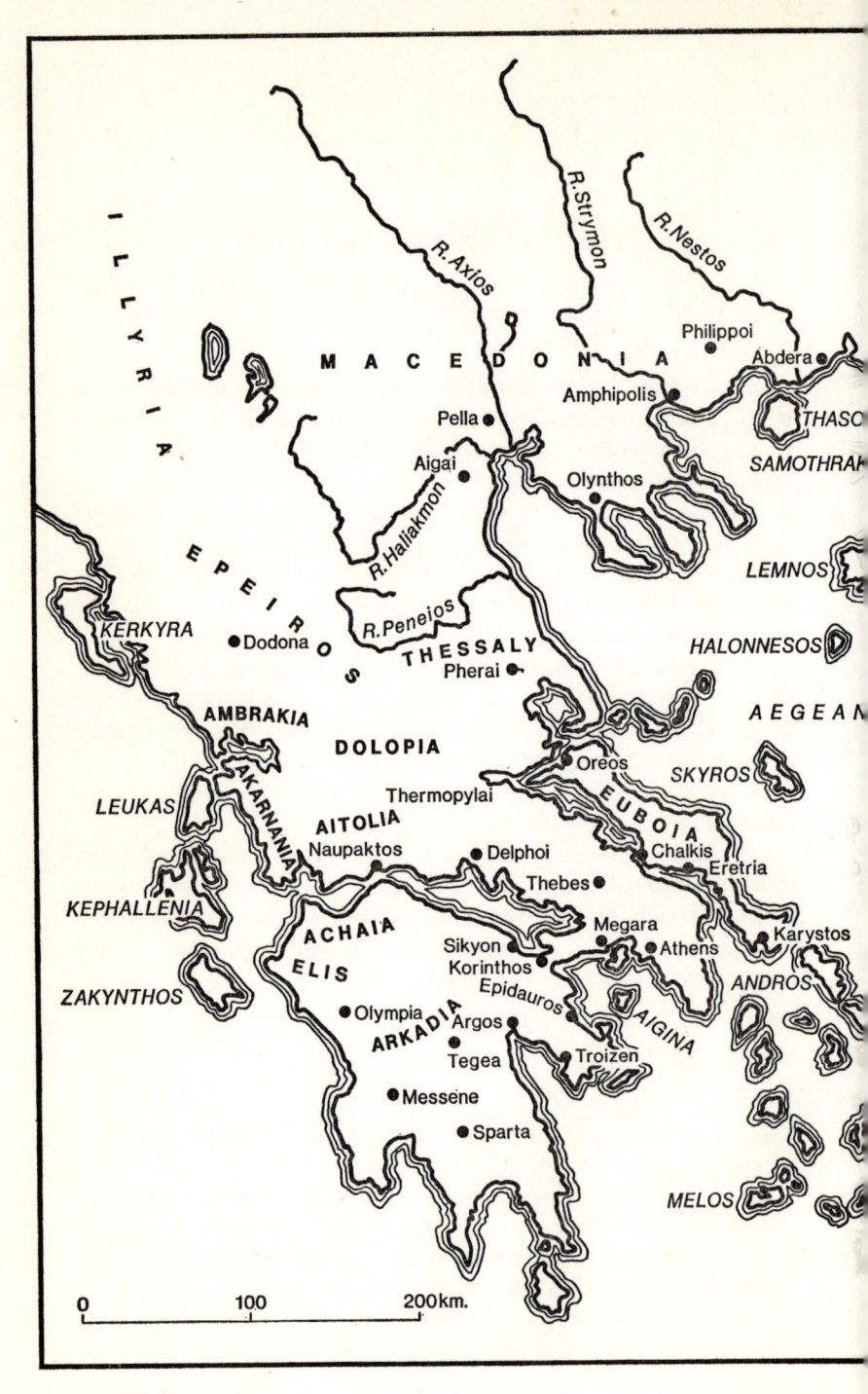

Map 1 The Aegean Area

Map

BLACK SEA

THRACE

R. Hebros

Maroneia
Ainos

Selymbria
Heraion
Ganos
Kardia
Lampsakos
Sestos
Abydos
Ilion

Perinthos
Byzantion

PROPONTIS

PHRYGIA

MYSIA

ASIA MINOR

LYDIA

IMBROS

AIOLIA

Mytilene

LESBOS

CHIOS

IONIA

SAMOS

TENOS

NAXOS

KARIA

KOS

LYKIA

RHODOS

'those from Alexander'. This however is not to be taken to mean that the king was regarded constitutionally as absolute ruler of the state – for there were certain qualifications to his power – but rather that circumstances had not yet arisen (or were in our period only now beginning to arise) to render inadequate the primitive concept of the king as the personification of the state. With the conquests of Philip, Alexander and the successors, with the dismemberment of the expanded state and with the appearance of several 'Macedonian' armies and several different king-commanders there first grew the pressing need of a more precise definition not only of the state itself but of the status of the king in relation to it. The confusion of the sources during this period of expansion and fragmentation (especially between 334 and the 220s),[3] during which theoretically national rulers acquired extra-national territory to which their claim as conquerors was automatic but which it will not always have been politic to treat as their private property, has given rise to some eccentric, legalistic theories, but these need not detain us here.

The origin of the monarchy is lost in antiquity but there is good reason for likening it to the Germanic chieftainship described by Caesar and Tacitus,[4] involving an elected military commander whose authority in peacetime was initially a function more of his personal standing and strength than of his office. Such systems may have gone back to a common Indo-European root.[5] By the time of the historical period, however, the Macedonian monarchy had evolved and solidified into something more formal but with residual traces of its beginnings. With such a theory in mind, as well as such features as the common informality between king and subject, scholars have often and rightly called the Macedonian ruler *primus inter pares*, presupposing origins in a system in which power pre-existing in the people is in a sense delegated to the king by acclamation, or *election* – as opposed to one in which power pre-existing in the person of the king is acclaimed or *recognized* by the people.[6]

In practical terms the king was leader in all military action unless he cared to commission subordinates to specific commands. He was chief priest, responsible for the religious obligations of the state and its people to their gods. Certain specified cases apart, he was supreme judge. But his power was limited – to an extent that no doubt varied according to the personal *auctoritas* of the individual monarch – by ancient law or tradition,[7] not necessarily the less real for being oral. In general this must have governed the proprieties of the king's actions with respect to his people and theirs with respect to him. It tended to restrain him from absolutism. In a difficult situation one of Alexander the Great's courtiers – not even a Macedonian – was to remind his leader that Macedonian kings ruled 'not by force but by *law*' –[8] this in a context where the king, by attempting to enforce on his own subjects the Persian practice of prostration, was in effect seeking to alter the legal (or at least the traditionally *proper*) relationship between ruler and subject. On the accession of a new king the Macedonians swore to him an oath of allegiance[9] and, if (in the absence of further evidence) we may judge by the similarly constituted, neighbouring Molossian state, this was an undertaking 'to serve (or guard) the kingdom according to the laws', to which the king responded with an oath 'to rule according to the laws'.[10]

There seem to have been two specific limitations on the powers of the ruler: he could not designate his own successor, nor did he have legal jurisdiction in trials for treason, to which he, the state, was a party.[11] As regards the former, the crucial question is whether the act of acclamation (*anadeixis*) by the army represented a form of selection or merely one of recognition. The aftermath of Alexander's death strongly suggests the former.[12] Although circumstances at that time were complicated by the lack of a clear successor the issue was resolved by an assembly of the whole army – or, rather, the expeditionary army then at Babylon. The leaders had their own various schemes and interests but the army as a whole was prepared and able to go its own way.[13] From the solution itself and from the expressed wishes of the army it is clear that there was a strong and natural preference for the nearest-born;[14] and no doubt under normal circumstances the eldest son always succeeded. But is is also evident that, as in this case where no clear-cut and obvious choice was open, the decision was in the hands of the army, however much it might be influenced by the machinations of the living or the preparations of the dead. Normally, that is, in practice this military power may have amounted to no more than a confirmation of what had been made inevitable by birth and training. But when no suitable prince was available it provided a mechanism for designating a successor from outside the immediate family. In the case of a king's death before his eldest son was old enough to rule it may have been normal nevertheless to acclaim the boy king and to appoint a regent-guardian – provided at least that there was not too long an interregnum to fill and that there was a suitable regent offering. But it must have been possible – and in this lies the only real difference between the Macedonian and a truly dynastic system – when extremely difficult circumstances made it imperative to find a successor mature enough and of sufficiently regal stature to command the kingdom's loyalty from the outset, to by-pass the natural recipient. As in the case of Philip II's accession this will have been an easier decision when the alternative to a very young son was a mature brother of the deceased.[15]

With respect to the jurisdiction of treason-cases, the king, through his personal authority and through the role he chose to play in the proceedings, might influence the decision, even practically put it beyond doubt;[16] but the judgement was not his. Obviously enough, he might investigate and prosecute a case of treason; as the state in person he was automatically, one would imagine, the plaintiff. But, as with the Roman Republican tradition described by Polybios, he (like the Senate) was responsible for the 'public investigation' while the people or the army (in Rome's case, the military assembly of centuries) was the sole judge.[17] In peacetime, according to Curtius, this function of the army was discharged by 'the people'.[18] While we can scarcely believe that in a country so dispersed as Macedonia any meaningful assembly of the people could be convened, we may perhaps take it that the reference is to the army organization when not actually under arms. As we shall see, it seems likely that no other national institution existed in any case.

HETAIROI

Around the king stood his people. In the military context, virtually the only one surviving, they appear to have been his Companions (*hetairoi*), the common soldiers and certain others referred to as the Macedonians of the camp[19] – possibly analogous to the Roman *capite censi* (*i.e.* citizens without property) and probably indigenous and enslaved subjects, serving as menials and camp-followers.

Unfortunately, the term *hetairoi* seems to have been used somewhat vaguely. It applied, for example, to a certain element of the army: the Companion Cavalry (or simply 'the Companions').[20] Near the beginning of Alexander's reign these must have numbered 3,300 or more, in as many as fourteen territorial divisions plus a so-called Royal Squadron.[21] But only a few years earlier it could be said by Theopompos that the *hetairoi* were no more in number than 800, that they owned large estates ('no less land than 10,000 of the richest Greeks with the largest estates') and that they included not only Macedonians but Thessalians and others from elsewhere in Greece.[22] They were distinguished – or they should have been, according to this most jaundiced of authors, who thought they were not – by their excellence. These were 'the Companions of the King', or 'the Companions of Philip.' The word thus seems to have a narrower and a broader sense – or perhaps a social and a military sense; from the noble, large-landowning class, whose heads of families were the king's barons, came also (from its younger men,[23] the sons and close retainers) the heavy cavalry force of the army. From the former came also the experienced commanders and administrators, a pool of talent on which the king drew for appointment to responsible positions.[24] It – or part of it – formed as well an inner circle, a council of elders who might advise the king and served as his personal retainers, very like the Homeric *hetairoi* or the *comitatus* in Tacitus' *Germania*.[25] It was a class which lived, fought and drank hard, which hunted and feasted for relaxation and whose interests – since, like those of the Spartans, its estates were tended by serfs – were primarily fostered by war.[26] During Philip's reign the *hetairoi* seem to have been swollen by numbers of new men, even non-Macedonians, whose status, conferred by the king, was confirmed by grants of land from conquered territories.[27]

SOLDIERS

The soldier-class, presumably the smaller landowners (in practice, perhaps, the remainder of the Macedonian citizenry), might serve the king as infantry – either in the regionally levied Foot-Companions (*pezetairoi*),[28] in the elite corps of Shieldbearers (*hypaspistai*)[29] or as light cavalry (*prodromoi*=scouts, or *sarissophoroi*=lancers).[30] In 334 the infantry component of the Macedonians under arms, both in Alexander's expeditionary force and in the home guard under Antipatros, was 30,000 or more, which included the 3000-strong Hypaspists (the Royal Bodyguard) and perhaps a total of twelve to fourteen territorial divisions of Foot-Companions.[31] The light cavalry were small in number; only 1000 or fewer seem to have served in the expeditionary army.[32]

SUB-CITIZENS

Of the lowest class we know even less.[33] There must certainly have been a substantial body of sub-citizens, increased hugely by the conconquests of Philip, serfs like the Spartan *helotai* and the Thessalian *penestai*, whose labours on the land made economically and socially possible the operation of large citizen armies over long periods. It will have been from this element and perhaps from lower citizen groups with particular non-fighting skills that the groomsmen, servants, wagon-drivers, labourers and camp-followers in general were levied.

ARMY AND STATE

These four divisions within Macedonian society are presented to us almost exclusively in a military context by sources whose interest in the kingdom, outside that in the king and his more immediate retainers, was exclusively in its military achievements. But, even allowing for this bias, it is surprising that we learn almost nothing of other aspects of this society. Perhaps in institutional terms there was no other aspect. Military service was a part of the citizen's obligation to his state – which is to say, to his king. The oath of allegiance, whatever its form, in all likelihood embraced this. But other liturgies were owed by people to state. After the battle at the Granikos in 334, Alexander buried the dead and to the surviving parents and children of the Macedonians he granted remission from three forms of liturgy: personal service (presumably the military obligation) and two taxes, apparently local and national.[34] Taxes had to be collected, and this was probably effected in local administrative districts coinciding with the regional divisions in which troops were levied. In Lower Macedonia, since the time of Archelaos, such towns as Pella, Mieza, Aigai, Beroia, Alkomenai, Pydna and Aloros and, in the territories annexed by Philip, such towns as Amphipolis functioned as regional centres. In Upper Macedonia, where the population was less concentrated, the administrative system was grafted on to the indigenous structures in the tribal principalities, Orestis, Eordaia, Tymphaia, etc.[35]

But there is no sign of any administrative class or of state officials other than the military-officer element, which raises the presumption that even in the regionalized post-Archelaos system the whole country and all its districts were administered through the military hierarchy – a 'civil' organization which drew its executives from the parallel military structure and took its orders, like the army, ultimately from the top, the king-commander-state. Thus when Alexander remitted what appear to be military and civil obligations they both fell in reality under the same military heading.

THE KINGDOM

Such was the basis of the tough, rugged and bellicose society forming an effective shield across the top of the Greek peninsula. It was a frontier society preoccupied with the survivalist concerns of a people obliged to defend a land of relative plenty against pressures from the massive tablelands and the precipitous valleys to the north. Its own frontiers were extremely long, like 'a great circle, the southeastern segment of which is filled by the Aegean Sea,'[36] and they had to be carved out and maintained by the sword and the spear.[37]

The western border at Philip's death – to establish the mise-en-scène of his reign – was formed by the high, rugged Pindos range and its outriders Mt Petrino running between the Lychnitis and Prespa lakes, and Mt Touria, farther north. The Pindos divides the major part of the Hellenic peninsula in half, into a northeast and a southwest, and level with the top of the Aegean it separated the Macedonians from their kin, the Epeirotes, on the Ionian Sea. From its northwestern extremity the border ran eastwards by Mt Babouna and the northern limits of the Erigon river plain, turning farther northwards as far as Stoboi, at the confluence of the Erigon and the upper Axios, farther eastwards via Mt Messapion and after crossing the Strymon it followed the south-easterly line of Mt Orbelos and thence across to the Nestos, which formed the eastern frontier. The southern limits were defined by the Aegean coastline, including the peninsula of the Chalkidike, as far south as Mt Olympos and the mouth of the Peneios.[38]

For the kingdom itself the starting-point must be the three great river-systems that water, to some extent define and in fact created Macedonia.[39] The greater inhabited part of this land comprises tertiary and quaternary alluvial plains scoured out by the passage of these rivers from the massive ranges that dominate the Balkan hinterland and deposited below them. The Haliakmon and the Axios together with the Loudias and the Echeidoros built up the Emathian Plain and continue to precipitate heavy deposits of silt in the Thermaic Gulf. Farther to the east are the Strymon, with its long, oblique plain dominated by the modern city of Serrai, and the Nestos, flowing southeastwards at the foot of the Rhodope massif and southwards to its marshy Aegean mouth. Farther east again, the Hebros similarly dominates Thrace. The primary characteristic of all these rivers is their 'European' or 'Continental' type, as distinct from their 'Mediterranean' neighbours south of the Peneios; they flow throughout the year without drying up or even drastically reducing their volume during the hot summer months.

The Emathian Plain, north and northwest of the Thermaic Gulf, has always dominated Macedonia on account of its central position, its size and the comparatively ready access from it into most of the surrounding areas – rather than because of its superficially impressive naval situation. In fact this gulf, like most of the northern coastline (with the exception of parts of the Chalkidike), is poorly protected from the southwesterly gales or from the northeasterly Etesian Winds (the Meltemi) that sweep down across the plains in summer and early autumn. The gulf, moreover, even nowadays presents sailors with difficulties caused by silting from the efflux of four rivers into its waters. The modern vessel of any appreciable draught is obliged to hug the eastern coastline above the Chalkidike to avoid sandbanks opposite the mouths of the Haliakmon and Axios, in spite of the advantages brought by modern dredging

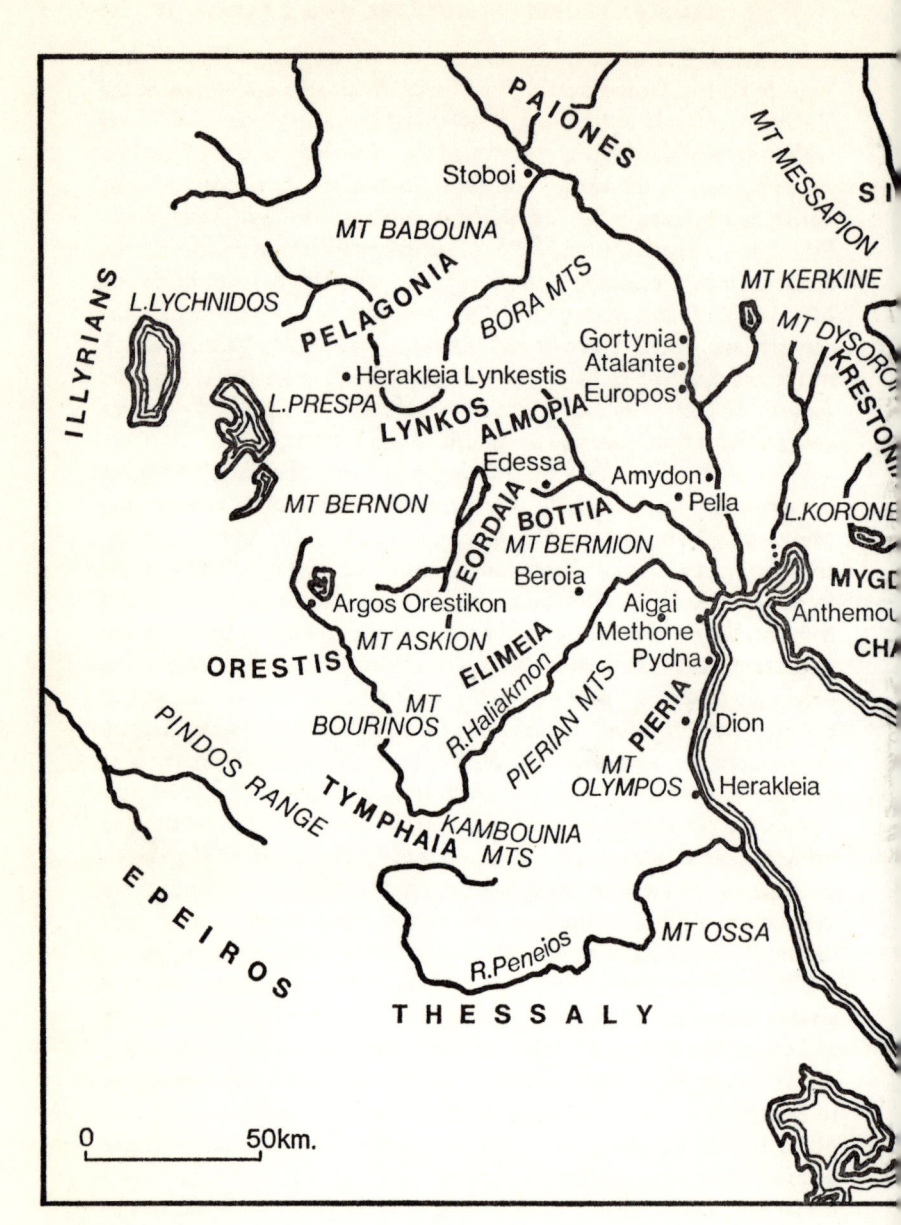

Map 2 Macedonia

RHODOPE MASSIF

IKE

THRACE

T MENOIKION
OMANTIKE EDONIS
R.Strymon   • Philippoi
              • Neapolis
SALTIA   R.Angites
          MT
• Amphipolis PANGAIOS   • Abdera
BOLBE
                    THASOS
• Stageira

DIKE
ynthos
         Akanthos
Poteidaia
Mende
kione
                                LEMNOS

AEGEAN SEA

techniques. Although the smaller ancient ship will have been less affected by this, the shallowness will certainly have contributed to the ease with which the waters were stirred up by the wind.

The Strymonic Plain, almost totally enclosed but for its narrow path between the hills at its mouth and the valley of the River Angites, which connects it with the inland Plain of Philippoi, is now the most fertile of the plains of Macedonia and Thrace; its significance in antiquity, however, lay more in its timbered and metalliferous environs. Except by the narrow coastal route the Strymonic Plain is approached only with difficulty from the west. The massive Krousia range and Mt Bertiskon extend from the low coastal hills for some 90 kilometres of almost impenetrable forest northwesterly to Mt Kerkine near Lake Prasias. On the east, except for the entry of the Angites valley, it is similarly shielded by Mt Menoikion, a continuation of the long Orbelos system and, near the coast, Mt Pangaion and Mt Symbolon.

The Plain of Philippoi (now dominated by Drama, 20 kilometres northeast of ancient Philippoi), is enclosed but for its connection with the Strymon. The only real passage to the east is that followed by the modern road from Kavala to its airport through the coastal hills. The plain was cleared and drained during the reign of Philip.

The plain of the lower Nestos may be passed over briefly. Only its smaller part – that west of the river-mouth – lay within Philip's Macedonia and in classical times it probably contained little more than marshlands. There is a conspicuous lack of ancient settlements on the coast between Neapolis (Kavala) and Abdera (near Cape Baloustro). Its main significance for Philip's reign is that the Nestos valley formed, with the Axios and the Hebros, one of the avenues of entry into the Aegean Basin from the areas north of Macedonia and Thrace.

West of the Emathian Plain three parallel mountain ranges run southeast and northwest, dividing western, or Upper Macedonia into two long, narrow series of valleys and small plains, the nearer drained by Lake Begorritis and its tributaries and the farther by the upper reaches of the Haliakmon. Both are terminated in the south by the Pierian and Kambounian ranges, which form the border with Thessaly, and in the north by Mt Babouna and its foothills at the top of the upper Erigon Plain and by Mt Touria, northwards of Lake Prespa.

THE ECONOMY

Thus the whole of Macedonia (as Philip left it) comprises a succession of five roughly parallel plains and valleys from the Pindos range to the Nestos, the broadest and most central embracing the head of the

Thermaic Gulf, and separated from one another by extensive ranges of mountains, penetrable only at intervals and not, especially in the west, without difficulty. The great bulk of the area is remote from the sea and little affected by it climatically – in marked contrast to more southern peninsular Greece. Winters, especially in the western uplands, are harsher and, especially nearer the coast, summers more oppressive and more unrelievedly hot than in the Mediterranean climate of Central Greece. At Monastir (ancient Herakleia Lynkestis) in southern Jugoslavia the January mean temperature is below freezing point and rises to 22°C in July, compared with coastal locations like Thessaloniki and Kavala, whose mean temperatures range from about 5°C to about 27°C with respect to the same months. In Athens the relevant figures are 9° and 27°.[40]

It is the fertility of the plains and the relatively high population-densities they sustain that account in large measure for the historical importance of the Macedonians, the frontier people of the Greek world. Cereals flourished (as they still do) in the large expanses available for their cultivation and horses, cattle, sheep and goats were grazed in abundance. Even now one-fifth of Macedonia is covered with forest and the mountains in antiquity were productive sources of timber and pitch;[41] the Dysoron-Bertiskon range and the high land of the northern Chalkidike in particular provided the best shipbuilding timber in Greece.[42] Game abounded. Herodotos mentions deer, boar, wild oxen and bears, as well as leopards, lynxes, lions and panthers.[43] Not unnaturally the hunt was a significant feature of the Macedonian economy and, for its youth, an important skill in the attainment of manhood. The man, however high-born, who had not yet succeeded in spearing his first boar without the aid of the net, was obliged, it is said, to sit at table instead of reclining with those who had established their manly prowess.[44] (In earlier days of lesser refinement, he who had not yet killed his first enemy was made to wear a halter instead of a belt.)

Copper and iron were available in considerable quantities and were mined and worked from the Late Bronze Age.[45] The same was true of gold and silver, the presence of which is attested from the silver mines of Damastion, north and east of Lychnitis,[46] to Philippoi in the Angites valley. Philip certainly mined the precious metal in the region of Mt Pangaion and in that of Damastion and very probably the silver mines of Mt Dysoron near Lake Prasias, which were first exploited by Alexander I, who derived from them one talent of silver per day.[47] The central town of the Pangaian area was Krenides, founded in 360 by Thasian islanders and refounded by Philip four years later as Philippoi.[48] The famous Asyla mines, which formed the basis of operations here and supplied undoubtedly his largest single source of revenue, were probably just east of Krenides, and returned an annual income of 1000 talents.[49] The principal other mining district near Pangaion was at Skaptesyle, south of the mountain and near the coast. It was said to have been owned at one time by Thucydides.[50]

With such resources Macedonia was self-sufficient. Such trade as passed over the frontiers was carried by land and the kingdom was in no way reliant on the sea. The population was large by Greek standards. When estimates must be based on the most indirect of information – arrived at mainly by extrapolation from military figures – clearly the imponderables are so great as to deter all but the foolhardy and the desperate. One has to guess first at the ratio of men under arms to the total military manpower available – done at best by analogy with other societies often hardly better known; then multiplication by a factor of 3½ or 4 may give a very general approximation to the total citizen population. This may in itself be a useful exercise, though its results can be expressed only in heavily qualified terms. But as regards the total population the larger problem for Macedonia – like that of the slaves for Athens and Rome – is the size of the subject element, those largely Thracian tribes that were not driven out at the conquest and occupation of their territory but apparently remained, some of them, to work the soil for their new masters. This 'rural proletariat' has been estimated as high as three fifths of the total population in 334, the only date for which we have moderately secure figures for men under arms.[51] Some control over the figures may be exercised by estimating the bearing capacity of the land,[52] but it is to be stressed that the following suggestions should be regarded only as the most general of indications.

POPULATION (IN 000S)

Adult male citizens
- under arms in 334 35
- not under arms in 334 .... 50 – 60

Total 85 – 95

Sub-citizens 50 – 80+

Total adult males 150+

TOTAL POPULATION 500+

THE MAKEDONES

During the eighth and seventh centuries, as the result of a quite remarkable surge of expansive energy early in that period that has left archaeological remains far afield,[53] Illyrian tribes dominated the bulk of this area later to become Macedonia. One important site illustrating their presence – probably as a ruling military caste – is that near the neighbouring villages of Vergina and Palatitsa, on the foothills of the Pierian range overlooking the southwestern corner of the Emathian Plain, inland some 20 kilometres from Methone and seven or eight south of the banks of the lower Haliakmon.[54] Here the archaeological picture is of constant Illyrian occupation from c.800 BC until around the middle of the seventh century. Although this is only one of many such known to the excavator its importance – first of all, no doubt for its strategic situation – is noteworthy in the development of Macedonia. Farther southwards, on the slopes of Mt Titarion and the Pierian Mountains, together the northern extensions of Mt Olympos, were located the Makedones, giving their name to the area, Makedonis.[55]

In the early seventh century the Illyrian tribes occupying the northwestern corner of the Aegean area retreated quickly – for their roots were not deep – before a series of Thracian and Paionian thrusts, themselves under pressure from Kimmerian migrations southwards from southern Russia into the regions east and west of the Propontis.[56] The Illyrian strength contracted westwards and northwards towards their original (and later) homelands but they continued to occupy at least the uplands of western Macedonia-to-be, where they intermingled with the Molossian tribes that had survived their earlier expansion.[57]

EXPANSION

The Makedones somewhere near 650 BC became subject to a new and foreign ruling group claiming descent from the Temenid family of Peloponnesian Argos (a claim accepted in antiquity by both Herodotos and Thucydides as well as by the officials of the great festival of Olympia).[58] Their arrival is described by Herodotos[59] in a picturesque version which may have been circulated by the conquerors themselves to camouflage their dependence – in the assertion and perhaps the maintenance of their authority – on Illyrian assistance, for it was by way of Illyria that they had come and the Illyrioi still retained overlordship of this area, as the archaeological record at Vergina shows.

It was under this leadership, headed by Perdikkas I, the first of the dynasty of these Argeads, that the expansion of the Makedones began, probably in a movement northwards for the short distance to the southern bank of the Haliakmon. The Illyrian site at Vergina was taken and a capital established at this impressive point, ideally situated for a commanding view across the river and over the plain beyond. It was named Aigai, 'the place of goats' – a Delphic oracle later blessing its foundation in canting terms as 'the gift of aigis-bearing Zeus', a fertile place of flocks and 'gleaming-horned goats'.[60] During the century down to *c.* 550 BC the Argeadai Makedones extended their sway farther northwards over the areas of Bottia, Eordaia and Almopia. Driven before them the existing populations – or parts of them – migrated elsewhere, the Pierians apparently to the region of Mt Pangaion and the Bottiaioi into the hinterland of the Chalkidian peninsula. The Eordoi barely survived, their remnants settling at Physka in Mygdonia. The Almopes were similarly expelled, so we are told.[61] What we should understand, probably, is that while there were refugees there also remained a proportion of the original population as subject inhabitants of the conquered lands. The growing kingdom now stretched from west of Mt Bermion northwards to the Bora Mountains and eastwards to a narrow corridor held by Paionian tribes down the basin of the Axios. Beyond the river until the second half of the sixth century lay Thracian-dominated regions.

During this century of the rise of the Kingdom of Emathia the rule, according to tradition, passed successively through the hands of Argaios, Philippos I, Aeropos I and Alketas. But in the second half of the sixth, under Amyntas I (*c.* 540–498), the kingdom was extended and superseded. During his reign Macedonian domination extended as far as the mountain range bordering on the north of the Chalkidike, with the consequent annexation of part of Mygdonia, the valley of the Anthemous (the town or area of the same name was offered as a refuge by Amyntas to the exiled Athenian tyrant Hippias in 510)[62] and probably the narrow Paionian strip along the Axios (Amphaxitis).

Alexander I (*c.* 498–454), son and successor of Amyntas, increased the kingdom in the wake of the retreating Persian invasion-force to include the areas of the Krestones and Bisaltai, replacing their Thracian overlord. The territory of the Argeadai Makedones now extended northeastwards to Mt Kerkine, which bounds Lake Prasias on the north, and eastwards to the River Strymon – the whole of the area later described by Thucydides as Macedonia proper – as opposed to the related and allied but autonomous western uplands of Upper Macedonia.[63]

THE UPPER MACEDONIANS

It is unlikely that the Makedones had been sufficiently numerous or powerful to exert much influence on the upland tribes, among which an Illyrian element remained, but of which at least the southernmost were probably closely related to the Epeirotic tribes on and across the Pindos range.[64] But by the time of Thucydides 'the Lynkestai, the

Elimiotai and the other tribes of the uplands' were *Macedonian* (and elsewhere he refers to the first-named as Lynkestai Makedones).[65] It is thus clear that in the first three-quarters of the fifth century some degree of Macedonian power had made itself felt in the west – either, that is, during the reign of Alexander or in that of his successor Perdikkas II.

The evidence is slight, but these beginnings appear to be attributable to the former; and in this region too he may have profited from the Persian invasion of the Greek mainland. Apart from the likelihood of some penetration from Pieria into the more southerly uplands by Xerxes, which will ultimately have been to the advantage of his Macedonian 'satrap',[66] there are some signs of the establishment of a relationship from about this time between Elimeia and the Argead ruling house. We are told that a certain Derdas (apparently Derdas I, king of Elimeia) was the son of the Elimiote king Aridaios and was also cousin of the two sons of King Alexander I (Perdikkas and Philippos).[67] This presumably means either that Aridaios, himself an Elimiote, married a daughter of Amyntas I of Macedonia, or, if he was an Argead (which is more likely, since his name is common in the family), that he ruled the princedom with an Elimiote wife, who bore him Derdas, his successor.[68] Whatever the truth of it, the contact is clearly there, and it may even be a case of the temporary annexation of this upland region by the Argead kingdom; and it must date roughly to the time of Xerxes' campaign. If the influence of the central kingdom was not yet expanded farther north and northwest into Tymphaia, Orestis, Lynkos and Pelagonia, then at any rate it was by Thucydides' time. And if the inference is justified that such new relationships were born in enmity and distrust then that is consistent with their continuing pattern.

Significant are the terms in which Thucydides speaks of these associations: the uplands are, in his time, Macedonian in a sense – some allied and some subject – but they nevertheless retain their own rulers, unlike Lower Macedonia, which is under the rule of Perdikkas II.[69] These loose bonds amounted at best probably to mutual recognition of territorial limits, occasional treaties of friendship and, no doubt, at times the temporary acknowledgement of overlordship or of independence. Their troublesome and ephemeral nature may be seen in the attempts of the same Perdikkas (*c.* 454–413)[70] to subdue a recalcitrant and powerful Lynkestian monarchy, attempts made certainly with and probably also without the aid of the Spartan Brasidas.[71] A little earlier, after the revolt of Poteidaia from the Athenian Empire, the Athenians had exploited this divisiveness by enlisting the aid of Perdikkas' brother Philippos, along with Derdas I of Elimeia, in a campaign directed against the Macedonian king.[72]

In 382 Derdas II of Elimeia served in alliance with Amyntas III on the Spartan side against Olynthos.[73] Phila, probably the daughter of this prince, married Philip II either shortly before or shortly after his accession.[74] But such relationships were interspersed with the sort of enmity exemplified in the Elimiote alliance with Athens in 432. During the reign of Archelaos the king was forced to separate the Elimiote monarchy from his Upper Macedonian and Illyrian enemies by contracting a new marriage alliance.[75] Seventy years later, at the fall of Olynthos to Philip, among the prisoners taken was another Derdas, the king's own kinsman by marriage, brother of Phila.[76] He had probably gone into exile at the time of the king's marriage to his sister, whether in Philip's reign or in that of his predecessor, when Elimeia may have been finally annexed to the Argead kingdom. Of the Orestian monarchy we know almost nothing.[77] But we are better informed as to the sharp antagonisms traditionally dividing Lynkos and Pelagonia from the plainsmen of Lower Macedonia.

During the Peloponnesian War the Lynkestian king Arrhabaios seems to have been periodically at war with Perdikkas II, and this was indeed the normal state of affairs. Symptomatic of the fierce independence of this mountain monarchy was its proud claim to Korinthian Bakchiad descent.[78] While temporary agreements were occasionally expedient — for example, Arrhabaios appears as a friend and ally of the king in the Athenian/Macedonian treaty of 423/2[79] — he was certainly at war with Perdikkas around 418 and with Archelaos a few years later.[80] (On the latter occasion the Arrhabaios in question may have been the son of the former prince.) A Pelagonian, Menelaos, son of Arrhabaios, became and remained an Athenian citizen during the late 360s and the 350s, when Athens and Macedon were at war; he contributed aid and money to Athenian attempts on Amphipolis, which were being resisted by Perdikkas III.[81]

From the little information available to us it is of course impossible to trace relationships between the two Macedonias with any precision at all. But what we can say with some confidence is that almost whenever the activities of the upper kingdoms impinge on the attention of our sources — whether for this very reason or quite incidentally to it — the picture is markedly one of tension, mistrust and outright enmity. In Lower Macedonia the larger populations planted crops on the fertile plains; they lived a comparatively settled life on and around the estates of the Macedonian nobility and the king. In the western mountains, by contrast, the Upper Macedonians must have depended more on pasturage, with the rugged, shifting life-style that implies, in a harsh environment in which the transhumance of livestock is still practised.

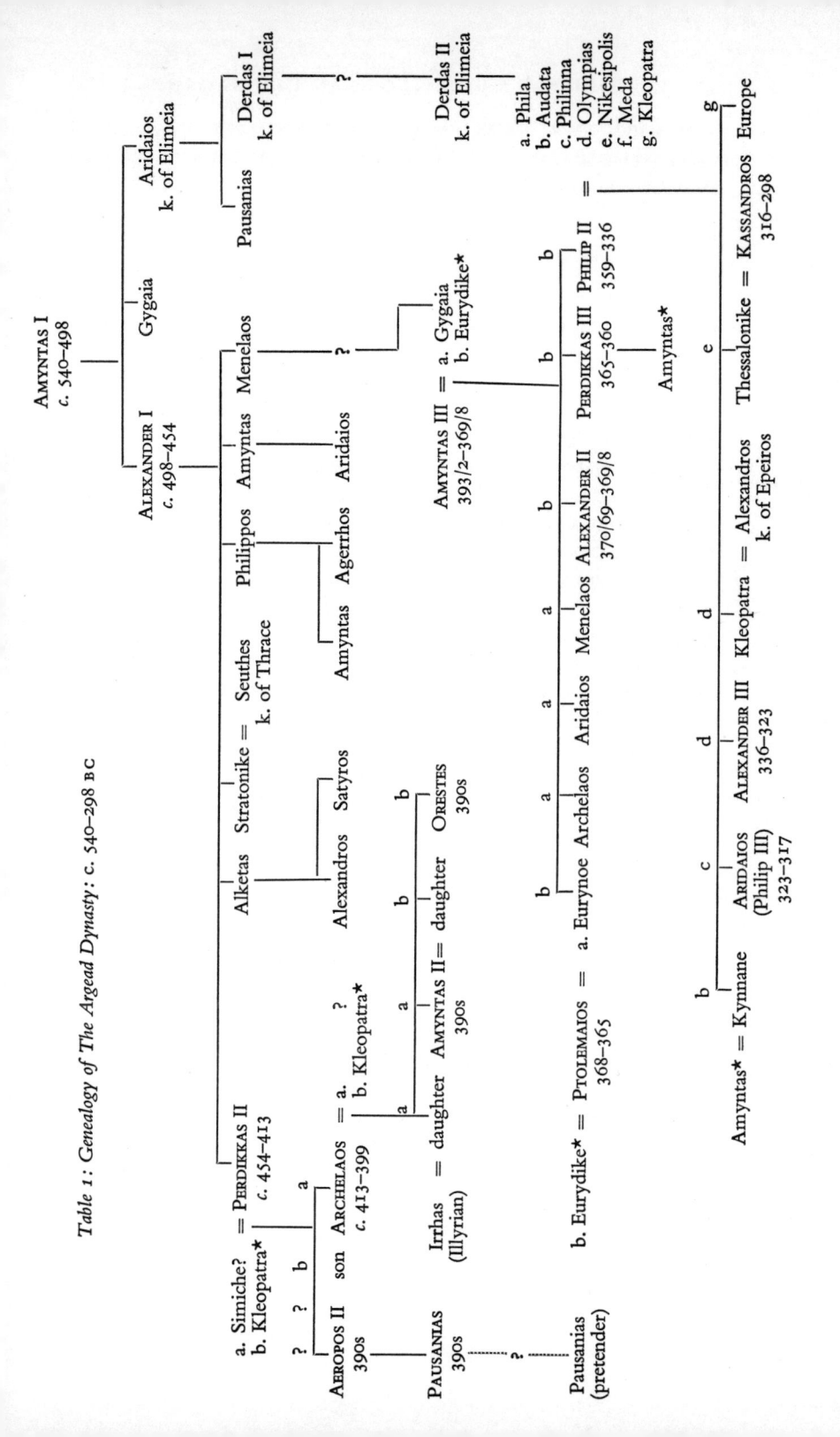

Table 1: Genealogy of The Argead Dynasty: c. 540–298 BC

They lived a ruder life in smaller, more isolated communities, much more akin in many ways to the Illyrian tribes with whose fringes they were intermixed.

KING ARCHELAOS

Towards the end of the fifth century, then, Argead influence had extended intermittently into these western areas, but the important achievement of the previous decades had been the growth of the kingdom towards the east, as far as the Strymon. It was to some extent in acknowledgement of this that Archelaos (*c.*413–399), the son and successor of Perdikkas, removed his seat of government to Pella – although Aigai long remained the spiritual capital, burial-ground of the Argead kings and venue of some of the great occasions of state.[82] Pella lay northwest of the Thermaic Gulf on what was at that time either an inland extension of it or an inland water formed at an intermediate stage in the development of the gulf as silting impeded the access of the River Loudias to it.[83] Ideally situated with regard to the sea, yet (because the naval approaches from the gulf must have lain either up the river or through narrow and shifting channels in flat, marshy land) not especially vulnerable to seaborne attack, Pella, at its establishment as the capital, nevertheless provoked no Macedonian movement on to the sea, even though this was the period, at or just after the end of the Peloponnesian War, when the breakdown of Athenian power left a temporary vacuum between the shores of the Aegean. (Among the northern states it was the trading cities of the Chalkidian peninsula that profited from the Athenian decline.) Macedonia was a country whose resources were adequate to its needs and the economic basis and motivation upon which navies are built simply did not exist. Not until the reign of Philip II was any attempt (known to us) made to build a fleet, and that very limited in scope. Archelaos' motives must be sought elsewhere.

His new capital was more centrally placed in the extended kingdom, better insulated against incursions from the southwestern frontiers. The king may have been especially concerned at the proximity of the two Greek colonies, Methone and Pydna, with the latter of which he was at war early in his reign.[84] But there is some reason to believe that Archelaos' accession was dubiously achieved[85] and it is possible that he was also concerned to raise a new power-structure dependent on his own patronage away from the long-established nobility clustered about the old Argead court. Within a generation Pella was the largest Macedonian city.[86]

The kingdom was anything but homogeneous. During the acquisition of the original areas of Pieria, Bottia, Eordaia and Almopia, its kernel, although large bodies of pre-Macedonian occupants may have been expelled or slaughtered, one tribe or a small group of tribes from one part of Pieria could not fill and defend so large a space; indigenes in large numbers must have remained there in alliance or subjection to the newcomers. Expansion eastward of the Axios by the time of Perdikkas II had added diverse groups of Paionian, Edonic and Thracian stock. The kingdom was a conglomerate of tribal territories interspersed with small settlements acquired piecemeal over many generations. There can have been little sense of cohesion.

The response of Archelaos, so we may infer from indirect evidence, was to reorganize Lower Macedonia into a series of cantons dominated by and perhaps administered from central towns[87] – and it is perhaps also in this context that the transfer of the capital belongs. His attempts to strengthen the military capacity of the state probably accompanied the broader reform, with the new centres serving as agencies for recruitment. According to Thucydides there were, before the time of Archelaos, few strongholds and fortresses in the country; it was in his reign that the bulk of those known to him were constructed (presumably, therefore, late in his period of exile.)[88] Good military roads were built and the kingdom was generally organized more efficiently for war by provision for 'cavalry, arms and other equipment beyond what was achieved by all eight of his predecessors'. It was apparent to the Athenian author that the military capabilities were uneven; the cavalry was excellent (though perhaps not numerous) but the infantry was totally inadequate. Thus Perdikkas II, when meeting a Thracian invasion led by Sitalkes in 429, had not even considered levying the infantry forces but based the defence entirely (and on this occasion successfully) on his horsemen. It is likely, if we picture a Macedonian society comprising a pre-existing peasantry subject to the Makedones themselves, that a feudalistic structure combined with an agrarian economy could hardly produce anything, in territory eminently suitable to horse-breeding, but a horseborne landowning class together with an under-equipped motley of peasants and serfs.[89] The implication of Thucydides may be – though this is arguable – that Archelaos gave his attention not only to the cavalry, which was already effective, but to the creation of a proper infantry from the smaller landowners of Macedonian stock;[90] but the traumas of the decades to follow, which must have largely erased any advance he may have made in that regard, preclude any certainty.

Archelaos also – apparently to a more remarkable extent than any of his predecessors – deliberately fostered the spread of Hellenic culture, perhaps in the hope that it might override particularist local ideas and ideologies. Painters, musicians, poets – men of the stature of Agathon, Timotheos, Zeuxis, Euripides – travelled to his court.[91] It seems that in some ways the beginnings of a national identity, or at least the intention to establish one, may be attributed to this king. The more tragic then for the kingdom that its energetic leader was struck down in his prime with no heir strong enough to guarantee a stable succession.

ANARCHY AND INVASION

The state lapsed into near anarchy over the next few years. Orestes, the young and legitimate successor, was despatched by his regent Aeropos, who was followed briefly on the throne by his own son Pausanias[92] and, apparently at the same time, Amyntas II (another, younger son of Archelaos).[93]

The reign of Amyntas III began with the murder of Pausanias in 393/2. (Amyntas II was killed by the Elimiote Derdas.)[94] But although he reigned for 24 years this period was not as secure as its length might suggest.[95] His accession was the signal for an Illyrian invasion, against which the king contrived to strengthen himself through alliance with Olynthos, the powerful hegemon of the Chalkidian League.[96] But when the invasion came, probably in 392, it was so quickly successful that no help arrived. However, forced initially to abandon his capital, Amyntas was able, by making a grant of territory (probably including the Anthemous valley and the near-by area of Lakes Bolbe and Koroneia), to attract enough Olynthian assistance to regain control. Thessalian aid seems to have been involved. But the price of salvation was high. The Illyrians withdrew but on condition of an annual tribute, which continued for over three decades.[97] At about the same time Amyntas took as wife the Illyrian princess Eurydike, presumably as a further condition of peace.[98] Then, during the 380s, the alliance with Olynthos turned sour and this decade saw the installation of a rival king, Argaios, almost certainly the creature of the Olynthians, who ruled in opposition to Amyntas for two years (c.385–383) before he was expelled; at the same time Olynthos expanded so far into Macedonia that even Pella itself fell under its power. Only Spartan intervention between 382 and 379 restored the king to his capital and the lost territories to the kingdom.[99]

THE SONS OF AMYNTAS

Over the past century, since Argead authority had extended to the Strymon and into proximity to the cities of the Chalkidian peninsula and to Amphipolis, for which Athens still intermittently contended, Macedonia had become the prey of the major powers, Athens, Olynthos and Sparta. Vulnerable on its western and northern flanks to Paionian and Illyrian penetration and unable, for lack primarily of internal cohesion (for the efforts of Archelaos had had no time to take hold), to utilize its manpower and resources in its own defence, Macedonia was incapable of pursuing a policy of independence. Amyntas realized this and, observing the renascence of Athenian sea-power in the early and middle 370s, aligned himself accordingly in 375 or later. In 371 at the peace conference in Sparta the Macedonian delegate relayed the king's acquiescence in the Athenian claim on Amphipolis, a clear sign that Amyntas was prepared to submerge his local interests in the hope that a stable relationship with the revived naval power would pay higher dividends.[100] But the battle of Leuktra soon destroyed that hope and during the 360s the Macedonian kingdom swung back and forth between Athens and Thebes in their contest for northern influence. Indeed it soon emerged that the Athenians had insufficient interest in fulfilling treaty-obligations in the northern Aegean; the following two decades or so were to see a constant policy of unparalleled irresponsibility on the Athenian part, in which alliances were contracted without any real hope (or even intention) of carrying out the warranties assumed under their terms.

Alexander II (the first son of Amyntas and Eurydike), after a brief foray into northern Thessaly, relieving his ally Larisa from occupation by the troops of the tyrant house of Pherai but remaining to outstay his welcome, was pushed back by the advance of the Theban commander Pelopidas and retained his throne at the price of Theban alliance and the surrender (among other hostages) of his younger brother Philip.[101] Within the next year he was dead at the hand of his brother-in-law, Ptolemaios of Aloros, who married the queen mother, Eurydike, and reigned technically as regent for her second son, Perdikkas. During this reign there seems to have been a temporary renewal of alliance with Athens, for we hear of the intervention of Iphikrates to prevent an attempt on the throne by a certain Pausanias.[102] But a second northern campaign by Pelopidas in the summer of 367 brought Ptolemaios back into line with Thebes, which is reflected in his combination with the people of Amphipolis to resist Athenian ambitions there. At the renewal of the Theban alignment Ptolemaios was obliged to hand over fresh hostages and at this time the young Philip was restored. He had been in Thebes between 369 and 367. He was aged 13 or 14 at his surrender and 15 or 16 at his return and we can scarcely credit the stories circulated by some ancient and modern authors that learnt and developed at this time many of the military ideas with which he was to inculcate the Macedonian army a decade and more later.[103]

In 365/4 Perdikkas (the second son of Amyntas III and Eurydike) killed Ptolemaios and followed him on the throne. Later in his reign the anti-Athenian stance hardened to the extent that in the face of strongly renewed efforts by successive Athenian commanders to take Amphipolis Perdikkas allied himself with the threatened city, supplying troops for its defence.[104] The combination was successful and, since Athens' antagonism towards Olynthos was too strong to allow her to seek assistance from this quarter, she proved herself ultimately incapable of recovering her strength in the northern Aegean.

Confidently – overconfidently – Perdikkas now turned to handle the perennial enemy, the Illyrians. The tribute imposed by the Dardanians on his father had been continued by his elder brother and probably by Ptolemaios.[105] Following what was apparently a minor triumph in the northwest the young king mobilized his forces for a major strike against the Dardanian king, Bardylis, and the two armies met in battle.[106] The new optimism of the Macedonians was dashed. After the battle four thousand troops and the king lay dead. The victorious Illyrians began to mass for invasion. The Paionains of the upper Axios valley took the opportunity to plunder and pillage in their vicinity. Since the dead king's son was as yet very young, at least two claimants to the throne materialized to oppose Philip, now 23 years old, the youngest son of Amyntas III. His major rivals, Argaios and Pausanias, received backing from foreign powers which hoped to capitalize on the confusion.

Such, in early 359, was the inheritance of Philip II. None of his difficulties was unusual in Macedonian history, though rarely if ever had a new king faced such a barrage of them. In the ensuing years Philip was to find means of dealing with the external enemies of the kingdom. But no less serious and much more basic to the security and wellbeing of the state was the fact of its own disunity, the geographical, historical and possibly ethnic discontinuity between east and west, between Upper and Lower Macedonia. To remedy this would be not only to build a firmer defence against outside interests but to unleash a driving national energy that would in the end lead the Macedonians with remarkable success very much further afield than their present narrow but threatening horizons.

CHAPTER II

359–357

THE ATHENIAN ALIGNMENT

PHILIP'S INHERITANCE

THE DEFEAT OF PERDIKKAS by the forces of the Dardanian Bardylis could hardly have dashed more abruptly the Macedonian optimism that had provoked the clash.[1] Four thousand Macedonians lay dead with their young king. Depression lay heavy over the country, for not only was the external threat to Macedonia more immediately serious than for at least three decades, but the dead ruler's natural heir, his son Amyntas, was no more than a child. Enemies of throne and state on all sides gathered themselves to pounce. Paionian tribes in the north, never so well organized as to present a real threat in times of relative stability but now for the first time showing sufficient unity to boast an overlord, Agis (whose successor, at least, was to mint coinage in his own name),[2] began pressing downwards along the Axios valley in search more of plunder than of conquest; this was seen by the contemporary Ephoros, whose account of these first years is circumstantial and credible, as a sign of their 'contempt' for the Macedonians. The victorious Illyrians,[3] already occupying probably a substantial area of western Macedonia, began to mass for a concerted thrust to the heart of the kingdom. Old claims to the throne were revived and encouraged. Athenian hopes rose at the prospect that in the confusion a puppet might be installed who would aid rather than hinder their attempts to recover Amphipolis; their candidate was Argaios, almost certainly he who had ruled briefly in the late 380s as the creature of Olynthian expansion.[4] To the east a Thracian king, probably Kotys,[5] advanced his interests by supporting the claim of another exiled pretender, Pausanias, certainly the one who had tried, under the somewhat similar circumstances of 368, to seize it for himself – again, probably, with Chalkidian backing.[6] Seldom can any state have so nearly approached total dismemberment without utterly disintegrating.

But there was a respite and it proved enough. Perdikkas, at some time after the return, probably in 367, of his remaining brother Philip from hostageship in Thebes, had decided to establish the younger man in a command of his own.[7] Whether this amounted only to a grant of estates which would support him and a household of retainers and guards, or was the creation of some form of 'dukedom' is unknown (as is its location), but it is tempting to see here a connection with the marriage of Philip to the Elimiote princess Phila, daughter of Derdas II.[8] In 348 we find Phila's brother, another Derdas, among the Macedonians' prisoners at Olynthos.[9] His action in leaving the country (at a date unknown) and joining its enemies was possibly prompted by his displacement by Philip from the Elimiote throne. Since Phila, by her Macedonian and regal birth, ought to have enjoyed a high status at the Macedonian court and since, on the other hand, no more is ever heard of her, we should expect that she was married either very early in the reign, dying shortly afterwards, or before it began, in a marriage that did not survive the link with Illyria through the marriage with Audata (359) – or perhaps that she simply produced no child. Elimeia thus rates fairly highly as a candidate in the very tentative efforts to identify this land allocation. It was far from the blandishments of power at the court in Pella and at the same time strategically situated athwart the important inland passes between Macedonia and Thessaly.

Such a cession, wherever the land, was no doubt a gamble, there always being the chance that Philip might have used these resources to precipitate his own accession. At any rate, fortunately in the event for his country, he was able to assert successfully his own claim to the throne and was acclaimed King of the Macedonians.[10] When the decision of the army was called for, Philip was not the only possible candidate. Argaios and Pausanias can hardly have presented themselves, since, after their respective activities in the past, they must have lived in exile, as is confirmed by their appearance at this time in league with foreign interests. Three elder stepbrothers of Philip – Archelaos, Menelaos and Aridaios, sons of Amyntas III and his earlier wife Gygaia – were alive and may have been in the country in 359, though it is unlikely that they were serious claimants on the army's attention. It is probably later that the eldest, Archelaos, gave cause or pretext for his liquidation and the pursuit of his brothers.[11] But the most obvious contender for the crown, and under normal conditions its natural recipient, will have been the young Amyntas, son of Perdikkas III.[12]

As we have seen, while in practice the military assembly may normally have simply confirmed the succession of the eldest male son, it nevertheless could act otherwise. It might appoint a regent and guardian, or, if the natural heir were particularly young, it might presumably set him aside altogether – as the nine-year-old Philip V was later to be set aside in slightly different circumstances but by the same authority. In 359 the son of Perdikkas was at the most eight years old; he may, and this seems more likely, have been no more than a few months.[13] And if the assembly was as a rule guided by the custom of dynastic continuity, it did have the power to break this normal chain, such critical circumstances as those of 359 presenting the strongest justification for doing so. The young Amyntas was passed over, though he remained alive throughout Philip's reign, enjoying a position of some stature[14] – which we should lay to the credit of the confidence induced in the new king by his own industry and success and the undisputed high regard in which he was held by the majority of his vast subjects.

THRONE AND FRONTIERS

Philip's new role was unenviable, literally beset as he was on all sides; not at all the situation to inspire in him at this early stage the monumentally ambitious schemes sometimes attributed to him. However, in his handling of the immediate difficulties and his concurrent concern for the long-term problems he demonstrated from the outset the skill that continued throughout his reign to win him success.

The first requirement was time. It is unlikely that Perdikkas in 360/59 had been able to levy substantially more troops than Philip collected in 359/8, so that those now dead represented probably one third and possibly one half of the available manpower under arms. Of the survivors a great many, like defeated soldiers past and present, must have drifted away to their homes, frightened, dispirited and content only to cling to family and property as inconspicuously as possible. Curiously, delay was granted by the Illyrians, and this was crucial; but some explanation must be sought as to why Bardylis, recently victor in such decisive terms over the Macedonian army, did not press his advantage; not until more than a year later – and then on Philip's initiative and not his – was battle again joined. Ephoros (through Diodoros) recounts explicitly the Macedonian fears of what was to follow from this quarter and comments that Philip took over a Macedonia 'enslaved' to the Illyrians, and yet he offers no reason for so vital a delay. It seems necessary to surmise the negotiation by Philip of an armistice with his neighbour. At about this time, presumably in either 359 or 358 – that is, either before or soon after his Illyrian victory broke this Illyrian 'enslavement' – Philip took an Illyrian wife, Audata, probably the niece or daughter of Bardylis.[15] On her marriage the girl is said to have adopted the name Eurydike,[16] one which after the trail of blood and Illyrian associations left by her namesake (probably her cousin or aunt) was not likely, we may suspect, to be of Philip's choice. But if the marriage and the name were forced upon him then the likely date is early 359, when Macedonia would have been obliged to beg for terms, and not 358, after the defeat of the Dardanians, when any conditions laid down would have been at Philip's pleasure. The daughter born by Audata, Kynnane, remained at Pella to be married eventually to Amyntas Perdikka,[17] but the mother does not appear again in any source. If the marriage-alliance was contracted in 358 to seal the new peace then it was remarkably ineffective, because in only two years the contracting states were again at war. On the other hand, if dated to 359, such a treaty, including the marriage-bond, would explain the delay over this crucial year during which Philip was able to establish his own position, meet the most pressing internal problems, conciliate Athens and defeat the Paionians. No doubt such a treaty was humiliating, though in that regard hardly new to the Macedonians, but it was also necessary.

Dardanian honour was assuaged, for Bardylis in his extreme old age had re-established with a vengeance the now customary superiority of his tribe over the Macedonians; tribute payments were no doubt resumed and guarantees of submission received. We may only guess at other terms of the treaty. In all likelihood substantial areas of Upper Macedonia remained in enemy hands, especially Lynkos and Pelagonia, perhaps not without some co-operation from the local nobilities, and it is possible that guarantees were extracted regarding the Illyrian status there. Such conditions were little more than Bardylis had sought in the past, and they were now again sufficient. For Macedonia they provided a respite.

AMPHIPOLIS AND ATHENS

At the same time, it being plain that the most urgent Athenian contention involved the ownership of Amphipolis and that the Athenians were prepared to back their ambition with money and men, Philip withdrew from Amphipolis the military aid supplied by his brother and with gifts and promises beguiled the Paionians into a temporary peace.[18] At his accession Amphipolis was at least technically and probably in fact autonomous,[19] so that Ephoros' assertion that he withdrew from that city 'after first declaring it autonomous'[20] needs to be interpreted as an affirmation of its existing status. Sixteen years later in the Athenian Aischines' catalogue of Macedonian ingratitude and Athenian forbearance, in which we should expect over- rather than understatement, the orator can say only that Perdikkas 'fought on behalf of Amphipolis against our city'. Clearly, his action had entailed not the garrisoning of a subject city but military aid supplied to an ally, which Philip now simply recalled – hardly, as Demosthenes was to claim and as others have since thought, tantamount to an actual cession of the territory to Athens, since it was neither his to give, nor theirs, without first taking it by conquest, to receive.[21] This is, however, not to say that Philip's intention was not to create an impression of philathenian benevolence – that indeed was the whole point, for he urgently needed Athens' alliance – and he followed up with a request for a formal declaration of peace between the two states.

With the Athenians cogitating and the Paionians for the time quiescent, Philip was able to turn to his eastern frontier, whence the challenge of Pausanias came. With his Thracian and possibly eastern Macedonian support, known for his earlier attempt on the throne and for his royal blood, Pausanias must have appeared to pose a serious threat. But once again, promises and bribes were sufficient to undermine the endeavour. Philip appears to have entered into communication with Kotys before the latter's death and may even have travelled to meet him personally at Onokarsis.[22] Since the accession of the one and the death of the other fell in close sequence and, therefore, there can have been very little communication between them, it is very likely that the object of this intercourse was Pausanias, who was, in the event, abandoned and killed by his erstwhile supporter. The tripartite division of Thrace on Kotys' death[23] and the consequent struggles among his successors put paid for the time to any further Thracian ambitions in Macedonia.

In Athens the newly improved prospects of success over Amphipolis had the effect Philip wished on opinion there, and, far from the substantial support that might have been expected to follow any signs of success in Argaios' quest for the throne, the Athenians now hesitated over whether to abandon the Macedonian exile. Before receiving Philip's overtures, they had dispatched a force of 3000 hoplites with naval support under the command of Mantias,[24] but his orders were now evidently countermanded. Argaios was landed at Methone, a pro-Athenian Greek enclave on Macedonian soil and there virtually left to his own devices; Mantias and the bulk of his force remained at Methone while Argaios with his own mercenaries, his fellow exiles and it seems a few Athenians, perhaps volunteers from among the hoplites, set out for Aigai where they hoped to win favour. It is interesting to see, in view of Demosthenes' later accusations of duplicity on Philip's part over the whole question of Amphipolis, that the Athenians at that very time, finding promise in both of these horses, were cannily hedging their bets. Since Philip, as the man in control, was presenting a friendly aspect, official aid was withdrawn from his rival; but, in case of Argaios' success, the Athenian troops were close at hand to assist in his consolidation and to remind him of his obligations.

Making his way inland to the west, the pretender marched his supporters the 20 km or so across the northern foothills of the Pierian Mountains to the old Macedonian capital.[25] In strategic terms this was a well-situated base, commanding the northward-facing slopes with a useful view across the Haliakmon and the southern extent of the Emathian Plain, and dominating, with Methone, the southern coastal approaches to the kingdom. Further, as the old capital, Aigai may well have contained groups of potentially dissident noble families whose power had been eroded by the transfer of power to Pella some forty years before. Some such explanation seems called for by Argaios' hopes that without even resorting to force he might win over this city to his cause. But such hopes proved vain, and he began his retreat to Methone. With, at most, only 25 km. (each way) to travel there had been every chance of his escaping, if necessary, before Philip's forces could be mobilized and brought down from Pella, a good 60 km. away on the northern shore of Lake Loudias. But he had underestimated Philip's speed of movement or his ability to anticipate, for he was intercepted before reaching the coast. It is in fact very difficult to approach Argaios' likely route in secret from the northern side, most of his path lying across slopes commanding the whole panorama of the plain across which pursuit must come, and it may be that Philip was already in his area. At any rate, the surprise on top of the failure at Aigai was decisive and the royal forces had no difficulty in defeating the pretender, carefully distinguishing in the fighting and in the negotiations that followed between Argaios' mercenaries, many of whom were killed, the Macedonian exiles, who were taken prisoner, and the Athenian volunteers, who were released without ransom and with compensation for their losses.[26] Argaios at this point disappears from history.

By the middle of 359, then, Philip's standing as leader of the Macedonians is already high among his countrymen, his initial achievements, in keeping with most of those to follow, being characterized by an economy of military effort balanced – indeed, made possible – by skilful diplomacy and delicate timing. The loyalty of the people of Aigai had been considered suspect, at least by Argaios, but their choice – that between the younger brother of the dynamic Perdikkas, whose abilities were already becoming evident and who had in particular caused formidable Athenian support to melt away, and the pretender, whose only real chance of success had been at spear point – had been, in the event, a simple one. Philip's first known military engagement, although his opposition may not have been very impressive, had been an unqualified success and must have helped raise the army's morale.[27] In Athens, opinion, once hostile and then undecided, solidified in favour of the proffered peace. The withdrawal from Amphipolis and the deliberately generous treatment of the prisoners taken near Methone had advertised the attractions of Philip as ally rather than enemy, so that the alternative attraction of alliance with Olynthos and its league won little support among the Athenians.

The Olynthians in fact were surprisingly late starters. Quick in the past to press their northward interests, their first known appearance in 359 was as rival suitors in Athens when that city was already debating Philip's peace-offer (although it is just possible that they had been backing Pausanias' claim on the throne). We are to take the two bids as alternatives, of which Athens, in choosing one, must reject the other. As Demosthenes said, when support for the Macedonian agreement was gaining momentum, some Athenians were even for expelling the Olynthian envoys from the city – though he did not say whether they actually suffered any more than the refusal of their request. For the Chalkidian League the issue was important. Although they can not yet have seen in Philip's Macedonia much more of a danger to themselves than it had been in the past, which was negligible, two of his activities must have given them cause for disquiet. His overtures to Athens, if successful, might well hem in the Chalkidian peninsula between a hostile Macedonian hinterland and an equally hostile Athenian sea. Further, if nothing more, the military reconstruction taking place across the frontier must already have thrown into jeopardy their important link with the silver-mines at Damastion, on which they had for decades been dependent for bullion.[28] Relations between Athens and Olynthos in the past decade had been unsurpassedly bad, and no doubt the former's unwillingness to accept the bona fides of so sudden a change of Chalkidian heart as well as the attraction of the new Macedonian king's overtures combined to produce the favourable Athenian response.

But their decision was not taken in ignorance and we err if we read it as the cynical hoodwinking of a naïve and gullible populace. Cynical it may have been and expedient it was, on Philip's part; on that of Athens it was no less so. In a costly war even a temporary advantage was worth pursuing, however little either side was likely to fall into the trap of guileless belief in the other's beneficence.

It is possible that we have part of an Athenian record of the preliminaries to the treaty in a few lines of an inscription apparently praising ambassadors from Macedon at a date early in Philip's reign, presumably in response to messages of goodwill.[29] As to the terms of the treaty itself[30] there is some doubt, hingeing largely on the meaning of Demosthenes' words: 'by saying that he would hand over Amphipolis and by cooking up that much bandied-about secret he won over our simple souls right at the beginning . . .'[31] It is most unlikely, as we have seen, that Philip straightforwardly recognized the Athenian claim to Amphipolis, for, whatever Demosthenes might assert here and elsewhere, the fact that Aischines failed to remind Philip of such a concession (or even to pretend later that he had done so), when he had no reason to suppress it and every reason, in support of the case he was making out, even to exaggerate,[32] must militate conclusively against it. But if Philip neither promised to hand over Amphipolis, because it was not within his power, nor acknowledged an Athenian right to it, he had, by his withdrawal, at least tacitly foreshadowed such recognition.[33] Probably some Athenians mistook the inference for the intention and very likely Philip carefully compounded their misapprehension with noncommittal encouragements. It is in any case unlikely, we may conclude, in spite of the vacillations of his predecessors on this subject, that Philip had to pay a high price for this peace; in a theatre where failure had followed failure the Athenians would find joy in any gain. All that was required of the Macedonian – and all, according to our best source, that he did – was to withdraw his military aid from the city and to affirm its independence of him.[34]

THE ARMY

The peace established, Philip was sufficiently relieved of external pressures in the late summer of 359 to devote his energies to border problems and perhaps to continue the military build-up he had certainly already begun. Ephoros' account (in Diodoros) of the first months of the reign lays heavy stress on the action taken by the king to reorganize, arm and train the Macedonian armed forces. In particular he singles out the infantry for mention.[35] We need not imagine that the evident transformation of Macedonian military capacities was anything but an arduous, expensive and protracted process; and it certainly took place over a good many years. But in view of the massive blow to manpower and morale suffered so recently, it is very likely that Philip gave much of his time at this stage to military matters. This is, therefore, an appropriate point to look briefly at some aspects of the subject. Although we are moderately well informed of the characteristics of Alexander the Great's army and are often justified in assuming that these were fundamentally the king's legacy from his father, we are on much shakier ground when we arrive at the task of assessing whether

Philip's responsibility for them was as innovator, reformer or merely transmitter. Just as, to the Athenians, practically every decree enacted outside living memory had to be Solonian, so there has been a tendency among modern as much as ancient authors to attach every pre-Alexandrian military feature to Philip.

The first clear achievement of Philip in this area was his very substantial expansion of the army. In part this was no doubt made possible by an increase in population, itself a product of the stability and security of Philip's reign, but in large measure it must have amounted to a realization of the hitherto little-tapped potential of the kingdom. Little is known of the army, especially of the infantry, before 359. The *pezetairoi*, according to Anaximenes (a contemporary, who should have known the current version), had been founded by Alexander I, a king whose expansive military efforts were by no means negligible.[36] In the century following his reign, however, not only does their title appear in no source but (and this may be the explanation) the only surviving references to infantry suggest that this first act of organization turned out, in the longer term, ineffective. The infantry remained a virtual nonentity. Nevertheless it was possible for Philip in 358 to levy 10,000 foot under difficult circumstances, and Perdikkas had presumably led as many against the same foe eighteen months earlier. When Philip is credited, therefore, with the virtual creation of the Macedonian phalanx[37] we are presumably to take this as an allusion to remarkable advances in size, training and technical sophistication – but not, even mistakenly, to the foundation of the *pezetairoi* themselves.

The *hypaspistai* are equally unknown to our pre-Alexander sources. Theopompos, writing during Philip's reign, seems aware of their function but – if so – misnames them *pezetairoi*.[38] But in spite of their late emergence into Greek awareness they were probably an ancient institution.[39] Originally, it is clear, they were a small foot-guard of the king; hence their occasional name, *somatophylakes* (bodyguards), which reminds us of their proper function.[40] They were a specially recruited force – distinct from the territorial levies of the Foot-Companions – chosen evidently (since their pay was higher) for their quality, and serving as the king's personal guard. By 334 they were 3000-strong, arranged in three chiliarchies, distinguished from the phalanx proper by their separate origin and recruitment rather than by any variation in armament,[41] and trained to serve in the new army, because of their smaller size, in a number of more mobile capacities.[42] As with their numerous fellows of the phalanx, they were not originated by Philip; but they were probably expanded in a similar way by him and trained in a new tactical use as the connecting link between phalanx and cavalry.

In 358 Philip raised 10,000 infantry and 600 cavalry to defeat Bardylis.[43] In 334 the grand total of Macedonians under arms was in the order of 35,000 with over 30,000 foot and 4000 horse.[44] Although the former figure was drawn from a smaller Macedonia than the latter it will presumably have represented, unlike that for 334, the heaviest levy the population could bear in the circumstances. So that, although certainties are out of the question, it is clear that over the period of Philip's reign a very substantial expansion of military resources had been effected. During Alexander's reign it was possible to spare substantial reinforcements for the expeditionary army without noticeably affecting the capabilities of the home guard under Antipatros.

High in the priorities of Philip's military programme must have been the provision of incentives and rewards at all levels. Most striking are the twin positions of the Companion Cavalry and the ('Companion') Hypaspists.[45] Both were élite corps in a special relationship with the king. Both could be regarded as royal. The Hypaspists' recruitment was presumably on the basis of excellence[46] – which is to say that their existence was an incentive to good service on the part of the *pezatairos* and a reward for his achievement. The same may have been true of the Companion Cavalry at a different level. Whether a high standard of service on the part of a light horseman could advance him to the *hetairoi* we cannot say. But Theopompos observed with surprise that the latter class (meaning the noble landowners) comprised not only Macedonians but Thessalians and other Greeks,[47] which means that Philip (that is, presumably he and not earlier kings) must have ennobled some of them. At this level, then, elevation was possible – even to the *hetaireia* – for the outstanding. The Companions, certainly, were levied by districts, but since these apparently depended on the location of the nobles' estates and those were granted (at least to new *hetairoi*) by the king, presumably as a concomitant of ennoblement,[48] this is no bar to our regarding the Companion Cavalry, like the Hypaspists, as an élite body to which access was possible from outside.

More usual inducements applied throughout the army, although our evidence for them relates only to the infantry. Arrian writes of 'double-pay men' (*dimoiritai*) and 'ten-stater men' (*dekastateroi*): 'the latter so called from their pay, which is lower than that of the *dimoiritai* but above that of the undifferentiated common soldiers'.[49] The pay-differentials arising from this passage and from an inscription-fragment probably of 336/5[50] (in which Hypaspist-pay is set at one drachma per day) appear to relate to three basic variations on standard infantry (*i.e.* *pezetairos*, presumably dr. 25 per month) wages: the Hypaspist rate at 30 per month, the ten-stater men at 40 and the double-pay men at

50.[51] These differentials were not for separate ranks; the lowest level of NCOs, the *dekadarchai* were superior to all of them (so Arrian). Apart from the prospect of advancement through the ranks, then, regular financial and status inducements were offered to the Macedonian soldier, in addition to the irregular emoluments of special bonuses and booty, such as Alexander later distributed.

These rates of pay are not Philip's, but presumably the status-differentials they reinforce were used by him. It has been urged that he had little need to spend money on his own soldiers, who were in any case obliged to serve him and might need sustenance only on longer and more distant campaigns.[52] And, if it is correct to assume that the Macedonian army down to the infantry class comprised landowners, large down to small, then the soldiery was in any case to some extent self-supporting.

But even with the use of mercenaries in later years to ease the burden of citizen-service[53] and allowing for the probability that Philip avoided heavier levies than necessary of the military classes,[54] still an appreciable call for service must have been made on the smaller farmer, who could less afford it. Yet only once do we hear of dissatisfaction among Philip's troops (although, had it been known to exist, Demosthenes would surely have delighted in reporting it)[55] and that was on account of a tactical blunder that cost unnecessary lives.[56] It seems justified, then, to conclude that the rewards for service under Philip, as under Alexander, were considerable. Macedonia's revenues were large and they were utilized to the full.[57]

We have noticed that land-grants were made to those elevated to the *hetaireia* and probably also to existing Companions.[58] The same benefits, it seems possible, were conferred on ordinary Macedonians, as Diodoros suggests when speaking of the division of Methonaian territory 'among the Macedonians' in 354.[59] To confer land on citizens was in some societies the best way of creating eligibility for military service, and this may well have been the king's aim; when it is remembered that the case for land-grants to *hetairoi* rests largely on a fortuitous fragment of Theopompos and on our knowledge of the areas represented by cavalry-squadrons,[60] it may be deemed a simple misfortune that, where the infantry are concerned, our sources mention (from a total of 12 to 14 recruitment districts) only three, and these by chance from Upper Macedonia. A fuller list might have allowed conclusions as to land-grants to the common Macedonians similar to those possible regarding *hetairoi*.

The inducements to wholehearted and efficient service were therefore very considerable and must have justified in the mind of soldier and officer alike the firm discipline and constant training and service demanded.[61] They served to bind the forces as a unit with its allegiance to its king-commander. In such ways an army was created that functions as a highly efficient and unified body. Developments made in the area of armaments were probably peripheral. Philip is said to have introduced the *sarissa*, a longer stabbing-spear. But on the whole his foot-soldiers were more lightly armed than the Greek hoplite, more akin to the Thracian peltast.[62] The heavy cavalryman carried a short sword, but his main weapon was a stout, iron-tipped stabbing-spear of cornel wood perhaps two metres long.[63] His armour, comprising iron helmet, some form of breastplate and protective padding (of bronze or leather) for the shoulders, neck and hips, and a smallish shield,[64] was much the same as that of the foot-soldier (except for the breastplate, which the latter did not wear). Although the bridle was in use, saddles and stirrups were not, so that fighting on horseback was a matter first of using the animal's weight and speed and then, once in contact, of the cut and thrust of hand-to-hand combat – rather than the armoured clash of mediaeval knights.

It was the use to which the heavy cavalry was put that distinguished Philip's army, especially in the eyes of most Greeks, to whom the horseman was an expensive luxury. The equestrian skill of the Macedonian troopers combined with the highly trained, relentless phalanx allowed the use of the latter as a base or pivot for all-out attack by the former, the striking arm. The Greek army, with its heavy, cumbersome line of hoplites, was no match for the variety of tactics open to Philip and his successors, although these are seen only in glimpses during Philip's reign itself, for the sources allow no more, but are clearly evident during that of Alexander.

PAIONIA AND ILLYRIA

In 359 much of this lay in the future and, in any case, probably counted in the end for less than the sheer confidence that flowed from victory after victory. As he prepared his forces to terminate the Paionian raids and for the important confrontation with the Illyrians of Bardylis, Philip knew that the most effective counter to the recent blow to the morale was a resounding triumph. When it came, at least, to the Illyrians, no quarter would be given and no prisoners taken.

The Paionian problem was not difficult and no doubt Philip tackled this first in order to train his soldiers against the easier opposition. There seems at no time to have been much interest among these inhabitants of the northern river-valleys in expansion southwards out of their fertile pockets.⁶⁵ Short-lived spells of military endeavour, brought about by the rise of an unusually strong chieftain, elevated by the zeal of his followers (and perhaps the ignorance of our Greek sources) to the status of king, could always be relied upon to subside into divided inactivity. Philip now availed himself of the death of one such leader, Agis, to launch an expedition to the north. Short and decisive it seems to have been, followed presumably by acknowledgements of allegiance by the defeated, recognition of frontiers and guarantees of military service when required. A small Paionian levy was taken to Asia by Alexander in 334, but we do not know when military service was first required of them. The Paiones, it is important to note, must inevitably play a significant role in Macedonian northern defences. Occupying especially the Axios valley, the main avenue of access to the Emathian Plain, these tribes represented a useful buffer on the fringes of Macedonian interest in that direction. Periodic demonstrations of military strength when necessary, but probably amicable relations on the whole, and the establishment of a string of fortresses at strategic points along the course of the Axios offered secure enough defence in that area, unless there should arise inordinate pressures from the populous Danube region beyond.

Either very late in this year or, more probably in the light of the harsh winter in this area, in the spring of 358,⁶⁶ Philip was able to reconsider his relationship with the Dardanian Illyrians with some degree of confidence in his rear. We have already had occasion to note the power of the kingdom of the Dardanoi, built up in the first four decades of the fourth century by Bardylis, now an old man of 90 years. The Dardanoi, one of the three most powerful Illyrian tribes (with the Autariatai and the Ardiaioi),⁶⁷ had been able through the weakness during this period of Macedonia and Epeiros to extend their influence southwards over Dassaretis and the important areas to the north of Lake Lychnitis, as well as westwards into Upper Macedonia and southwards into Epeiros – achievements sufficiently impressive to have attracted the alliance of Dionysios of Syracuse.⁶⁸

Philip's preparations, his mustering of 10,000 foot and 600 horse, must have given some cause for concern to Bardylis, for the latter initiated negotiations apparently in the expectation of an easy settlement;⁶⁹ but his only proposal for maintaining the existing peace was that both sides should retain the territories they already held. The Macedonians, he proposed, should be content to continue to endure the occupation of their northwestern princedoms. Bardylis' mixture of mild misgiving and over-confidence, totally misguided as it turned out, should make it clear to us that to a contemporary outsider, at least, Macedonian military strength was far less daunting than we might anachronistically suppose it.

The offer failed. Philip, obliged to bargain from weakness in early 359 was now prepared to test and demonstrate his strength. The armies, equally balanced in numbers, met probably in the Erigon valley close to Herakleia Lynkestis (near modern Monastir), a likely location in view of the cavalry Philip took with him into this mostly mountainous area. Seeing that the Illyrian centre was strong, Philip placed his picked infantry on the right wing, then, using his horse to harass the enemy flanks and rear, thrust forward against its left. As this began to fold, Bardylis drew his flanks in and back into a defensive square, which held for a time but eventually broke, his ranks fleeing the pursuing Macedonians. The battle plan here is interesting in that it is in marked contrast with those of Philip's and then Alexander's later battles, according to which the cavalry served an offensive role, with the infantry primarily an anchor or pivot. Although it has been thought on this count that the plan was not Philip's at all but possibly that of one of his leading generals, Parmenion,[70] this conclusion is not at all necessary, depending, as it does, on the unlikely assumption that Philip had been able by this early date to effect in substance the military reforms whose results on tactics are later so marked. The army we see in action here, as regards its numbers and mode of fighting, was hardly different from its predecessors, although the confidence in his infantry implied by Philip's assignment to it of so central a role may lead us to believe that retraining had already begun.

CONSOLIDATION IN THE WEST

The victory, in the course of which 7000 Illyrians fell, was significant, although it was won far to the south of the central area of the Dardanian kingdom. Philip annexed the territory of Bardylis in Dassaretis as far as Lake Lychnitis, which at once gave him a more easily defensible frontier to his northwest and effectively impeded further Dardanian incursions southwards through the valley of the Drilon. In order to strengthen this line he began, probably at this time, the process of disentangling the population groups in western Macedonia, which probably for decades had seen the admixture of Macedonian and Illyrian stock.[71] The dispersed Macedonian mountain-groups were amalgamated into communities based on the small plains, superficially at least more akin to the Greek *poleis* than to the scattered pastoral groups whose movements followed the seasonal needs of their stock. Such a process must have involved some changes to the local economy, since the more settled life introduced to these areas implies an agrarian rather than pastoral system. This indeed is a feature of the speech attributed to Alexander at Opis three decades later:[72]

> Philip found you resourceless nomads, most of you dressed in sheepskin, pasturing a few sheep on the mountain slopes ... he gave you cloaks instead of sheepskins, brought you down from the mountains to the plains ... and made you dwellers of cities ...

Transhumance of flocks, however, must have continued side by side with the new life, as it does to this day. Probably now too fortresses were dotted along the strategic passes to the northwest.

The Macedonians will hardly have believed that such measures would settle their problems finally on these frontiers; some resurgence of Illyrian and Paionian ambitions was to be expected, though it was perhaps unlikely to be so well concerted that periodic demonstrations of military superiority would fail to control it. However, some of the benefits were immediate. The most urgent requirement in the northwest and the west generally was for the reorganization of Upper Macedonia, and the relief of pressure won by these victories allowed that to be effected. The process has been regarded by some as an annexation, and in a sense this is so. But, as we have seen, the Upper Macedonian kingdoms had long been regarded as Macedonian and Philip will have been able to pose, with some justification, as the deliverer of his own people. The local princely houses and nobility had much to lose and some may have offered opposition. It may, for example, have been at this time (rather than before Philip's accession) that Derdas, probably an Elimiote prince, left the country; his appearance on the Olynthian side in 348 does not oblige us to suppose that his flight from Macedonia had taken him directly to that city.[73] In an inscription of 362,[74] a Menelaos the Pelagonian was named benefactor of Athens for his assistance rendered to Timotheos in the war against the Chalkidians and Amphipolis; he served, that is, on the side opposing his king, Perdikkas. Not long afterwards the same man was honoured by the city of Ilion in Aiolia as Menelaos, son of Arabaios, the *Athenian*.[75] It is possible, therefore, that this man (who may once have been Pelagonian king, but was certainly no longer so),[76] his period of antagonism terminated by Philip's annexation of the uplands, fled from Macedonia to receive Athenian citizenship.[77] The inscription from Ilion is not precisely datable, so that no certainty is possible, but since Philip could have expelled him before 358 and since Demosthenes' account of the matters appears to assign Menelaos' activities in Asia Minor to 359 at the latest, it seems more likely that he left Macedonia either voluntarily or as the result of pressure by the Pelagonian king[78] or, most likely, because he was driven out by the Argead king Perdikkas III, as the latter prepared for his campaign against Bardylis – a campaign intended *inter alia* to establish central control in the western uplands.[79]

The evidence for Upper Macedonian resistance, then, is far from certain. In the main, the few indirect indications we do have suggest that the local nobility, faced by superior power, took the line of least resistance and acquiesced in the annexation in return for recognized status in the enlarged kingdom – and perhaps, with it, a better vantage point from which the situation might be redressed in the future. Parmenion, who had possibly been king of the Pelagonians at Philip's accession, cast in his lot with Philip.[80] He is soon found commanding part of the royal army in his own area against Illyrians (356), and his status and influence throughout the reign are never in doubt. Three brothers from Lynkos – Alexandros, Heromenes and Arrhabaios, the sons of Aeropos – although they do not appear in the sources in the intervening years, are clearly powerful and influential men at the time of Philip's death; one, Alexandros, was by 336 married to a daughter of Antipatros and was a suitable appointee to the military governorship of Thrace.[81] The Perdikkas who became one of Alexander the Great's leading commanders and co-regent after his death was of the royal family of Orestis,[82] whence also came Pausanias, the member of Philip's bodyguard who stabbed him to death in 336.[83] The nephews of Derdas and sons of Machatas – Harpalos and probably Philippos and Tauron – who also occupied positions of stature in Alexander's army and administration, were probably from the royal house of Elimeia.[84]

But although this must have been a period of carefully planned activity – and the priority given it above other pressing problems accentuates its importance – it is likely that after the initial battle with the Dardanians large troop concentrations were unnecessary. And, in view of the inevitable trials of strength to follow, much of Philip's attention must have been given to the military build-up whose effects begin to appear within the next few years; in 356, for example, the army was to be capable of subdivision and simultaneous use on two different and distant fronts. Some reaction was to be expected from the Paiones and Illyrioi. From the Olynthians too, with Chalkidian access to the silver of the Damastinoi now closed off by central Macedonian control of the passes of Lynkos, reaction was likely. The mines of Damastion had now fallen under Philip's control and, although he allowed minting to continue there throughout his reign, new coin types reflect the change in ownership by the replacement of the ethnic by the names of two men, presumably administrative officials.[85] The eastern frontier at the Strymon was vulnerable to Thracian incursion –

a danger that could be considered no more than temporarily averted as a result of the division of territory and power within Thrace following the death of Kotys in 359.

THESSALIAN CONTACTS

Therefore, probably in late 358, Philip embarked on a flurry of diplomatic and other moves that were to complement the alignment with Athens already serving his interests. It is clear, although our sources give us little more than hints of its extent, that for decades there had been some understanding between the Macedonian Argeadai and the leading noble family of northern Thessaly, the Aleuadai of Larisa.[86] No doubt this link had been strained when Philip's eldest brother had attempted in 369/8 to retain under his own control the two cities he had delivered from the tyrant of Pherai,[87] but when an appeal came from the Aleuadai in 358 for assistance against the same enemy[88] this was the perfect complement to the aid certain Thessalians, probably they, had successfully advanced to Amyntas III, when in 392 he was temporarily driven from his country by Illyrian invasions.[89] Between the end of Philip's Illyrian campaign and his first-known contacts with Epeiros, that is in either late 358 or early 357, Philip accepted this plea and formed an alliance to resist the power of Pherai. Since our sources confuse this initial involvement in Thessaly with the definitive interventions of 353 and 352, we cannot be sure what commitments he contracted or actually fulfilled, though, in spite of his more immediate problems, he does appear to have supplied troops to his new ally.[90]

In keeping with what one source elevates to the level of policy, Philip cemented his treaty with the cities of the Thessalian League by marrying a woman of Larisa, probably a member of the Aleuad family.

OLYMPIAS

Then, at some time in 357, Philip contracted what was to become the most significant of his marriages, that to Olympias, who was a daughter of the late Molossian king in Epeiros, Neoptolemos. This arrangement, a natural enough link between the related Epeirote and Macedonian tribes, represented a successful intrusion into an alignment of some standing between the Molossians and Athens, and was to survive the disintegration of the latter's own treaty with Philip soon afterwards. In the 370s, Alketas, then king of Molossia in central Epeiros and educated in Athens, had entered the second Athenian alliance together with his son Neoptolemos.[91] On the former's death, the accession had been disputed, the army – which probably had the same powers in this regard as its Macedonian counterpart – placing both Neoptolemos and a younger brother, Arybbas, on the throne. By 357 Neoptolemos had died, leaving Arybbas king and guardian of his five-year-old nephew Alexandros.[92] Neoptolemos was also survived by two daughters, the elder, Troas, now wife of the ruler, and the younger, Olympias, probably in her middle to late teenage, now marriageable.

Although the marriage is represented in the sources as an *affaire de coeur*,[93] it was a bond expedient for both parties. Threatened and damaged, like their Macedonian kinsmen, by the expansion of the Dardanoi of Bardylis,[94] the Molossian overlords of Epeiros were impressed by Philip's great Illyrian victory and by the new treaty in force between their Athenian allies and the Macedonian king, and Arybbas was now content to ally himself also to the latter. For Philip too, during this time of reorganization in Upper Macedonia, the prospect was attractive, assisting, as it must have done, in the proper definition of the common frontier of the two states, at least by mutual agreement over the proper allegiance of the tribes occupying the Pindos slopes – though six years later this issue seems to have led to a serious dispute.

The Epeirote princess thus moved to the Macedonian court, at the latest towards the end of 357. In a polygamous situation there is no need to assume that she replaced Philip's existing wives, Phila, Audata and Philinna; neither the morality nor the politics of the occasion demanded it. Philip may have 'waged war by marriage',[95] but the wives he thus marshalled were not, as it happened, to be remarkable for their fecundity; Philip himself was to be deficient in the production of male heirs. Only two wives, Philinna and Olympias, bore sons, one each, to Philip, but that of the former was evidently mentally deficient[96] – and it is for that reason rather than out of diplomatic expediency that Olympias was later to enjoy the superior status accorded the mother of the heir apparent. It may have been that by this time neither of the first two wives remained on the scene. But whatever, if anything, had happened to Phila (and her crime, to judge by the silence of the sources, was that she was barren), and even if the Illyrian treaty sealed by Audata's marriage had been superseded, at least the latter's daughter remained at court to be married later to her cousin, Amyntas.[97] It is clear that, although among Macedonian royalty influential women were sometimes able to exercise power to an extent unusual in the Greek world,[98] the sins or deficiencies of the mother were not visited upon the children. (Rather, in reverse, the deviation of the offspring was likely to damage the parent.)

ATHENS' SOCIAL WAR

Meanwhile, outside Macedonia the Aegean power balance was in flux. It was apparent, following her recapture of Euboia from Boiotian hands in the summer of 357, that Athens, although in purely territorial terms her naval domination appeared impressive, was badly over-extended financially.[99] With the prospects of allied revolt looming, the Athenians took steps to safeguard their weak point at the entrance to the Black Sea by an alliance with the three kings of Thrace, Berisades, Amadokos and Kersebleptes.[100] But her actions of late had become increasingly reminiscent of her great imperialistic days of the fifth century, and, in the autumn, three of her more powerful allies seceded from her alliance. Joined shortly afterwards by Kos and with open aid and encouragement from the Karian dynast, Mausolos, the recalcitrants began to marshal their combined fleet at Chios.[101] After the heady success of their Euboian campaign,[102] the Athenians were quick to meet the challenge. However stretched their finances, this crisis faced them with the alternative prospects of seeing their whole alliance crumble before their eyes or of reconstructing the league convincingly enough to allow the reconstitution of its finances on a basis more favourable to themselves. For Athens the issue was crucial, and her attention and efforts must be wholeheartedly concentrated on it. Her northern and other interests, in so far as they were not involved directly in the allies' activities, would need to be pushed aside for the time being, for, dangerous as that might be, too much would hang on the outcome of the immediate war to allow any distraction from the achievement of her aims in it.

THE CAPTURE OF AMPHIPOLIS

If Athens' vital stake in the new conflict was not immediately realized, it was at any rate soon to become clear to the Greek world. Shortly after the return of the Euboian expedition, two Amphipolitans, Hierax and Stratokles, presented themselves in Athens before the *demos* with a plea 'to sail and take over the city' (as Demosthenes was to express it).[103] For such a course of action to have been even remotely plausible, the city must still have been free from Philip, but there must nevertheless be more than a little doubt over the orator's confidence that the Athenians, had they seized their opportunity, could simply have assumed control of Amphipolis there and then. The verb Demosthenes uses (*paralambanein*, translated above 'take over') is too indefinite in meaning to tell us, if we were prepared to believe him, whether an Athenian force would need to fight the inhabitants for possession (as they had already done in vain during six decades) or might simply accept it as a gift – though on grounds of sheer improbability the latter possibility should be dismissed, even if it is the orator's clear implication. It was to his advantage to parade this occasion as a simple opportunity missed. Demosthenes, as a matter of interest, did not call Hierax and Stratokles *envoys* (though Theopompos did).[104] But if they were officially commissioned and dispatched by the Amphipolitan *demos*, they were at any rate not *merely* envoys, for at least one of them was later to be among those exiled and outlawed after the fall of the city to Philip,[105] who is unlikely to have courted unnecessary unpopularity[106] or to have wasted his time by punishing mere instruments of the popular will. Hierax, Stratokles and presumably Philon and others must have represented a pro-Athenian or anti-Macedonian faction that feared Philip's growing strength more than distant Athens; but we must remain uncertain whether such a view was shared by the bulk of the Amphipolitans. This would presuppose a remarkably abrupt swing of opinion away from that which had welcomed the loan of King Perdikkas' troops[107] and which had fortified Amphipolis against Athenian designs for nearly two-thirds of a century.

No Athenian expedition was sent, by way either of pre-emption or, later, when the siege began, of assistance. On this count the case for acceptance of Diodoros' word in placing this appeal just after the outbreak of the Social War is strengthened.[108] The appeal, itself perhaps a desperate attempt to forestall any move by Philip to capitalize on Athens' new preoccupation, was unsuccessful because it was too late. Philip then struck, still reassuring the Athenians of his good intentions, but able now to choose the moment to preclude all chance of intervention; this campaign belongs in the autumn of 357, when the Etesian Wind (the Meltemi) will have made navigation at least problematical, or (more probably) in the ensuing winter, when it will have been impossible.

For Philip this heralded a substantial change in alignment, though it may be doubted whether he had wished it so. Over the past two or three years he had assiduously begun the task of creating a ring of buffers round the Macedonian kingdom. With Epeiros and the Thessalian League, with their developed (if, in the latter case, hard pressed) internal organization, he had established the beginnings of close ties. With the Illyrians and Paionians, both of which demanded military intervention, a firm definition of frontiers and establishment of military outposts, he had taken at least the first steps towards establishing Macedonian superiority. With Thrace, after buying off Kotys' support for the pretender Pausanias, he had as yet had no further need of dealing; the partition of the kingdom had temporarily removed any pressure on that front. The Athenian treaty of mid-359 had served to counterbalance, for the time, any threat from his naval neighbours of the Chalkidian peninsula.

Patently, no long-term and realistic Macedonian policy could be developed without taking account of Athens and the Chalkidian League. Athens' economic interests had involved her for more than a century on the coastline of the northern Aegean. With the Chersonesos and the Hellespont she must be concerned; and with the northern coasts, for reasons of trade and, in the end more vitally, for the security of her corn-route from the Black Sea, preferably so. But even though she excelled in that military area in which Macedonia was most deficient, the enmity of Athens alone was not an immediately serious threat to Macedonian security – unless her navy work in combination with Chalkidian wealth, harbours and hoplite manpower.[109] Philip's overriding need, then, where these two powers were concerned, would always be to prevent their collusion against him. In 359, the attempt of Argaios, and the determination implied in her backing of him, had driven Philip into the arms of the Athenians and the antagonism between the latter and the Chalkidians had left his neighbours antagonistic but temporarily alone.

However, the outbreak of the Social War drastically altered things. For although it is true, as many have seen, that this war was to provide substantial opportunities for expansion and consolidation for Philip, its initial impact was to deprive him of his most effective counter to Olynthian interests. Athens, whatever he might have wished, was no longer of use to him. Further, lest Athens should successfully re-order her allies and build for herself a new empire, he would need to act quickly in order to remove the bases she would then be in a position to use effectively in the furtherance of her interests and, inevitably, to the detriment of his own. From all points of view, then, the *entente* with Athens was finished. It is worth stressing, against the anachronistic view that Philip's intention from the outset was to increase his power progressively, step by step, until he stood at the head of the Greek world, that the initiation of this new alignment, which might be thought of as the second phase of his foreign policy, was brought on by the collapse of one of the major props of the first phase.

CHAPTER III

357–351
THE CHALKIDIAN ALIGNMENT

WAR WITH ATHENS

AMPHIPOLIS FELL BY STORM. After a series of assaults a section of the wall was breached and the Macedonians pressed through the gap amidst fierce fighting, during which many defenders were killed, until the last resistance subsided. This victory, with siege-machinery playing a significant role in its achievement,[1] marks the beginning of a long and successful Macedonian tradition; with the increasing sophistication of siege-equipment it became no longer exceptional that walled cities fell by direct assault.

Shortly afterwards the Amphipolitan *demos* issued a decree proclaiming the banishment and outlawry of Stratokles and Philon.[2] Ephoros, in a reference to the exile of Philip's opponents there,[3] claims that he treated the rest of the inhabitants considerately, suggesting, without actually saying so, that Amphipolis retained some of the forms of autonomy. This we might expect, since the Chalkidians had to be convinced of Philip's benevolence towards those who supported him; the form of the decree – a decision of the *demos* and not an executive order by the conqueror – reflects this, whether or not the assertion of autonomy was much more than a charade. At some time afterwards, Amphipolis was annexed and its territory ceded to Macedonians.[4] So, for example, by the end of Philip's reign the district served as a recruitment area for the Companion Cavalry. But the date of annexation is unknown, beyond that it took place before 336 and probably at some time after the conclusion in 356 of the Macedonian/Chalkidian alliance.

The Athenian declaration of war over Amphipolis followed immediately, but it was an empty gesture (especially since it must have coincided approximately with their defeat at Chios) and it was understandably ignored by Philip. He switched his attention to the coastal plain of Pieria and took the pro-Athenian town of Pydna. According to Demosthenes[5] the victories both at Amphipolis and at Pydna were won through the assistance of supporters within the walls. Pydna, like

Methone, was in origin a Greek colony[6] but, especially since its refoundation by Archelaos a half-century before, it may have contained a Macedonian element; but, even if not, there must have been those in the city who saw their safest course in maintaining at least a working relationship with the Argead monarchy, particularly now that its power was beginning again to look more firmly based. Treachery within Amphipolis too may have played a part in its fall, for the long and effective anti-Athenian tradition there must easily have conduced to pro-Macedonian sentiment. But, although we know no details of the means by which Pydna was taken, Ephoros, as we have noticed, is explicit in attributing the capture of Amphipolis to success in breaching its walls.

NORTHERN REALIGNMENTS

When Philip had needed alliance with Athens in 359 he had naturally given every impression of benevolence towards it; his actions at the end of 357, representing the transition to a new alignment, were similarly directed towards winning the confidence of his powerful Chalkidian neighbours. Some such reassurance was necessary, for the assault on Amphipolis had provoked a good deal of disquiet in near-by areas. The kings of Thrace, particularly, in the western region, Berisades and the sons who succeeded him at his death in the same year (357/6), saw it as a direct threat to their sovereignty. The Illyrian Grabos, ruler possibly of the Grabaioi, a tribe to the northwest which had apparently been able to expand to the Macedonian borders after the defeat of Bardylis' Dardanians,[7] was in communication at about this time with the Chalkidians, who agreed to form an alliance with him probably with the primary aim of recovering their connection with the silver mines of the Damastinoi. Negotiations, however, seem to have been broken off at a later stage[8] when it became apparent that Philip was prepared to bid high for Chalkidian friendship. Nearly three years before, Philip had ordered the abandonment by the Macedonian mint of the Persic coin-standard adopted by Archelaos and the reversion to the earlier Phoenician or Thraco-Macedonian standard in use among the members of the Chalkidian League.[9] This action, combined now with motions towards friendship, will have been taken to presage the restoration of Olynthian trading privileges within Macedonia, including those with Damastion.

Either in late 357 or early in the next year Philip stepped up his overtures to his neighbours, offering them alliance. Their doubts possibly already assuaged to some extent by the treatment of Amphipolis and the new enmity between Philip and the Athenians, their commercial magnates undoubtedly attracted by the new trading opportunities, the Chalkidians were won over by two additional undertakings: that Philip would assist them to take Poteidaia, which he acknowledged as the property of the league, and that he would cede Anthemous to them.[10] Poteidaia, anti-Olynthian, lapsed member of her league and stiffened in its opposition in 361 by the reception of a contingent of Athenian cleruchs,[11] was the most immediate source of discomfort to Olynthos; Anthemous, a Macedonian territory since the 470s but a source of dispute from time to time between its kings and their southern neighbours, lay to the immediate north of the Chalkidike, a rich and fertile river valley opening on to the Thermaic Gulf. They terminated their negotiations with Grabos the Illyrian and accepted Philip's terms. The arrangement is preserved, though without detail, in the fragment of an inscription set up in the Temple of Artemis at Olynthos and found there nearly forty years ago.[12]

PHILIPPOI

With this powerful alliance safeguarding his southern frontier, Philip was able to put into effect a strategy which aimed at the gradual elimination of the Athenian presence on the seaboard of Macedonia and Thrace. But the immediate initiative came from elsewhere, in the form of a request for aid from Krenides. Founded by islanders of Thasos in late 360 just to the northwest of the older Datos at the head of the Angites valley, eastern tributary of the Strymon, it was a base for the exploitation of the rich gold- and silver-bearing ores of the vicinity; this is reflected in the gold and silver coinage issued soon afterwards bearing the reverse legend 'Of the Mainland Thasians'. Such a wording indicates that the name Krenides had not been officially adopted; the foundation was initially no more than a collection of mining settlements. At the same time, the separate issue, distinct from that of the island Thasian coins, advertises the importance attached by its initiators to their new venture.[13]

In about May 356 the eastern Thracian king Kersebleptes seized the opportunity offered by the new military involvements of his ally Athens to trample on the agreement he had been obliged to sign in the previous summer with her and with Berisades and Amadokos.[14] Moving into the territory of the western ruler Ketriporis, son of Berisades,[15] he prepared to attack the Krenidean mining settlements.[16] Whether he was simply eager to re-unify for himself the kingdom his father had ruled or, perceiving that Macedonian sway now extended across the Strymon to Amphipolis, was acting to pre-empt any further move from that quarter we can only speculate. At any rate his action failed, merely providing an opportunity for Macedonian intervention. The Krenideans, finding themselves isolated among the weak and the unwilling, discovered in Philip a ready ally.

For the Macedonians this was a stroke of fortune. Krenides was located in a commanding position in the Angites valley, a mere 12–15 kilometres from the Athenian ally Neapolis (modern Kavala), though separated from it by the narrow range of hills running along the coast eastwards from Mt Symbolon. The area was well known to be rich in silver and gold and was capable of much more concentrated mining than had yet been devoted to it. The aid was given no doubt under the terms of a hastily concluded alliance[17] and it was successful. Afterwards the several communities, representing an ideal advance-post of Macedonian influence and defence, were drawn into one, renamed Philippoi (the plural form of the name, like the earlier, 'Krenides', probably indicating its originally scattered nature – and the allusion to the king who founded it setting a precedent for his successors) and heavily fortified with walls and towers. A large number of Macedonian colonists were settled there in order to stock a self-sufficient and defensible *polis*; apart from anything else, it might be some time before the surrounding territory would be secure.[18]

From the precious ores and, in particular, from the rich Asyla mines just to the east of the new colony, Philip was able by dint of more efficient extraction than before to draw annual revenues of more than 1000 talents. (It has been suggested that the increased productivity was due, at least in part, to the abandonment of tray-panning in favour of the use of long wooden flues with ribbed floors, into which the ore was shovelled after crushing by hammering. A water flow through the flues removed the lighter ore, leaving the heavy metal caught between the ribs.)[19] Whether this large revenue derived from outright ownership of the mines or from their lease is unclear.[20] Then, for the same reason as in the western uplands and elsewhere in Macedonia, possibly on the Emathian Plain itself, Philip made arrangements to stabilize the economy of the Angites valley (later known as the Plain of Philippoi) by the clearing of forests and the draining of the land. When the Thracians had occupied it, says Theophrastos, who may himself have visited it in the 340s, the plain had been full of forests and swamps, but now it was rendered cultivable; no doubt it was to till the soil that some of the Macedonian colonists were sent to the new city.[21]

The foundation of a colony was for Macedonia a new venture, one which however set the precedent for a long series under Philip and his successors. How many Philip established we do not know, but, as we shall see, at least one and probably several in Thessaly were to follow, and, in the late 340s, a number in Thrace. In immediate terms it was an invaluable source of revenue as well as an outpost against the Thracian kingdoms – those of Ketriporis and Amadokos as well as that of Kersebleptes. A new coinage with denominations in gold, silver and bronze, was issued by Philippoi under its new name, although its obverse and reverse types otherwise remained the same as before. It is generally believed that this autonomous coinage of Philippoi lasted only about a decade and a half,[22] but recent studies show that the mint continued to strike under its own name throughout Philip's reign and well into that of Alexander.[23] Since, by the time another decade had passed, all Thracian territory as far east as the Nestos had been annexed to Macedonia, such treatment of this one city is intriguing, representing the creation of a true colony and perhaps something of a showpiece. And, although it later emerged that its foundation had been a step towards the annexation of the whole area between the Strymon and the Nestos, the continuing colonial status of Philippoi is a useful warning against the unquestioning assumption that Philip's initial intentions coincided with his later achievements. In 356, it is clear, the most serious dangers facing the kingdom obliged Philip to concentrate internally on the unification of his diverse population-groups and externally on the fairly immediate safeguarding of its security by the formation of alliances with his neighbours. Philippoi formed a part of this pattern, in that it was akin to the forging of the Chalkidian, Thessalian and Epeirote links, an expansion of Macedonian influence beyond her own borders to establish buffers against more distant threats – particularly, in the longer term, against Athens.[24]

THE NORTHERN COALITION, RISE AND FALL

Such a step could not be taken, however, without immediate consequence. During probably the summer of 356 the initiative was seized by Ketriporis (the son of Berisades) in the negotiation of an alliance in opposition to Philip. He and his brothers won the support of Lyppeios, the Paionian successor to Agis, and of Grabos, whose Illyrian tribe[25] appears to have become stronger and more aggressive after the defeat of Bardylis in 358. These in turn were joined in July by Athens[26] in what, on the latter's part, could be no more than a display of sentiment, for by now she was pressed hard by her renegade allies and was in no position to honour new commitments. (By this time the rebels held Samos under siege. Soon afterwards, in the autumn, Athens was to transfer the action to the Hellespontine area, but this was born not out of success but out of a desperate need to distract her enemies from their Samian blockade.)[27] The strength of an enemy alliance of kingdoms to their northwest, north and east would have been very dangerous to the Macedonians, but the union of allies was not yet achieved and Philip moved quickly before their actions could be coordinated and their forces combined. Diodoros, in a brief notice of the campaign,[28] fails to mention Athens at all, either because he is referring only to the initial coalition before Athens joined it or because Athens played no part in its abortive activities. According to Diodoros' version Philip attacked the forces individually, terrified them and compelled them to join him. Plutarch,[29] in a tendentious context, mentions only the defeat of Grabos' Illyrians, which he attributes to a military victory by Parmenion. News of the victory – that is, its arrival at Poteidaia – he synchronizes with Philip's capture of the latter, with the success of the king's horse at the Olympic Games and with the birth of Alexander. Since the last is dated to July and the Olympics will have been held, as usual, in August or even September, clearly we must assume either that there were inexplicable delays in communication or (more likely) that later chronographers took liberties with their dates in order to manufacture an appropriately portentous context for the birth of Philip's successor. (Indeed Philip himself, or Alexander, may have first circulated the story.)

POTEIDAIA

Probably in about July Philip and his Chalkidian allies pinned down the Poteidaians under siege. (With no actual harbour but only a roadstead the city was vulnerable by land rather than by sea.) In spite of their other preoccupations the Athenians voted to launch a relief expedition but, as on several later occasions, the aid was too late; at this time of year the Etesian winds, as well as Athenian indecisiveness, may have been responsible.[30] The siege was soon successful and Poteidaia capitulated.[31] Although nominally autonomous[32] the city was completely dependent on Athens; it had been strengthened, as we have noticed, by the establishment there of cleruchs in 361.[33] At its fall these Athenians were allowed to leave and return to their own city without ransom. They were neither indigenes nor colonists but merely, as one orator was to say 'Athenians dwelling in Poteidaia'.[34] The same author, Hegesippos, was to claim[35] – to substantiate an allegation of Macedonian illegality – that the cleruchs were at the time Philip's allies; but his claim is false, since, as Athenians, their voice was not distinct from that of the Athenian *demos*, which was at war with Philip. Neither can his charge be interpreted to signify that the native Poteidaians were the allies in question, for any possible agreement between them and the Macedonian will hardly have been permitted by the resident cleruchs to survive the Athenian (and therefore their own) declaration of war at the end of 357. Hegesippos was merely indulging in fantasy in failing to admit that Philip's treaty of 359 with the Athenians had now been discarded;[36] he was the ally no longer of either the cleruchs or the Poteidaians. The latter, as willing hosts of enemy soldiers, were sold into slavery and their land handed, as promised, to the Chalkidian League.[37]

EXPANSION IN WESTERN THRACE

The foundation of Philippoi, as we have seen, posed an immediate threat to Neapolis, less than a day's march distant on the coast. A loyal member of the second Athenian alliance (as of the Delian League), Neapolis was a useful base for Athenian ships. Although on occasions nowadays its harbour may be unsafe for vessels of far greater seaworthiness than the ancient trireme (like most northern harbours and roadsteads it offered little protection against the strong winds that often blow up during the sailing season), it was at that time normal practice for vessels to be drawn up on the beach, so that such adverse conditions would only affect actual landings and departures.[38] The Macedonian presence at Amphipolis and Philippoi was shortly followed up by the destruction of Apollonia and Galepsos, both located on the coast at the eastern end of the Strymonic Gulf not far from Amphipolis, and by the establishment of a small Macedonian base, Emathia, on the site of Oisyme, only 20 km. west of Neapolis.[39] All three of these coastal towns were probably (Galepsos and Oisyme certainly) Thasian colonies in origin and at this time, as in the fifth century, found themselves, like their foundress, in alliance with Athens.

In the early summer of 355, according to an Athenian inscription, two Neapolitan envoys were received by the Athenian Boulē and commended to the assembly along with a bouleutic recommendation whose content is lost.[40] In spite of the disappearance of what may have been the most useful information on the stone it can hardly be doubted that the Neapolitans were reacting in alarm to the activities of Philip in their area over the past year. However, although their reception before the Boulē was clearly favourable, the envoys will have received little (if anything) other than expressions of sympathy. More than that the Athenians could as yet ill afford. The date of Neapolis' capture by Philip is unknown, but it may have been taken and garrisoned at some time between the end of Athens' Social War and early 353, only to be re-won temporarily by Chares near the latter date. It continued to issue its own coinage until nearly 340 – roughly the time at which Philip became master of Thasos – but if this was intended to imply autonomy it will have been a transparent farce after about 346 or even the late 350s. With the defeat of Ketriporis (along with Grabos and Lyppeios) in 356 the western realm of Thrace became, at the least, much more secure for the Macedonians and for their colonists at Philippoi, and, whenever Neapolis was actually annexed, the Neapolitans as well as the western Thracians will have found themselves thoroughly circumscribed by Macedonian influence by 350.[41]

THE END OF THE SOCIAL WAR

In the midsummer of the year 355, on the orders of the Persian King, Athens' Social War ended. The independence of Chios, Kos, Rhodos and Byzantion was recognized and the example of their secession was soon followed by the bulk of the remaining members, leaving only (of any note) the northern Aegean islands, Euboia and a few towns on the Thracian coast. The war, whose outbreak had obliged Philip to realign Macedonia with the Chalkidian League, had turned out well for him by engaging Athenian efforts elsewhere. There had been times during the previous two years when Athenian prospects had looked promising – when, for example, after her defeat off Chios her efforts had increased to a level at which she might well have defeated her recalcitrant allies and managed to convert her league, as almost exactly one hundred years before, into an empire. The immediate result of such a success would inevitably have been a complete reconstitution of the league's finances and an expansion of the imperialistic activities that had so concerned the Aegean states during the 360s.[42] Early in 355 Athenian hopes rose again after Chares' 'second Marathon' while in the service of the Phrygian Artabazos.[43] But in the summer, with the war ended, the Athenian cause abandoned and the bulk of the already inadequate *syntaxeis* lost, the Athenians were brought face to face with the reality of their exhaustion and their disastrous loss of prestige. The peace brought with it even greater encouragement to their enemies.[44]

ORIGINS OF THE SACRED WAR

Thebes, smarting over her defeat of 357 over Euboia, had seized the opportunity offered earlier by *stasis* in neighbouring Phokis to strengthen her position in central Greece, engineering the passage of two offensive decrees in the 356 spring meeting of the Amphiktyonic Council at Delphoi.[45] One was an ultimatum threatening holy war against Phokis if fines owed by certain individuals there, including leaders of the anti-Theban group, were not paid forthwith; the second censured all others owing debts to Apollo, these including the Spartans. If the intention was to encourage the Phokians, who had fought on the Boiotian side at Leuktra, to expel their anti-Theban element it backfired badly, producing the reverse effect of bringing that faction to the fore with apparently general support. One of them, Philomelos, was elected commander-in-chief of the army and, after receiving private assurances of money and mercenaries from Archidamos at Sparta, seized the sacred city of Delphoi in the summer of 356. During the following eighteen months, while Philomelos' troops consolidated their position and his envoys proclaimed the justice of the Phokian cause and renewed their ancient claim on the Delphic sanctuary, Thebes and Lokris took ineffective steps to dislodge the enemy from Delphoi, but were hampered by uncertainty over the Thessalian alignment from attempting to force the issue in the Amphiktyonic Council, where Thessaly could command a large majority of the votes. While the Thessalian *koinon* might normally be expected to vote against the Phokians, it was heavily preoccupied with the continuing struggle against the Pheraian tyrant house that had prompted it at least once already (in 358) to seek Philip's aid. During the last months of 356, moreover, Philomelos' diplomacy had won alliances with Athens, Sparta and some other Peloponnesian states, probably Argos, Sikyon and Korinth; with Athens' potential unclear the Thebans were unwilling to risk being caught between the other major powers.[46]

But with the close of the Social War the position suddenly altered. Thebes was left dominant in her area, allied to a Persian King whose apparent belligerence and whose successful determination of the Athenians' struggle counteracted the declining impact of his successive ultimatums since 387/6.[47] Athens was in confusion and unlikely to participate to any effect. In Thessaly too the situation changed. During 355, it seems likely, the struggle between the league and the tyrant house was active and perhaps prompted another appeal to Philip from his friends at Larisa.[48] The change of heart was thus possibly induced by a temporary settlement of the feud with (again, possibly) Philip's aid.

In autumn 355 the Amphiktyony declared holy war on the Phokians with probably the support of 18 or 20 of the total 24 votes.[49] In spite of the massive opposition, the position of Philomelos was strong. Ensconced at Delphoi and protected there by some of the more rugged terrain of the Greek peninsula he found his initially small resources now sufficiently augmented by funds from Apollo's treasury, enabling him to offer a mercenary wage half as high again as the normal,[50] so that he was able to go on to the offensive early in the following year (354).

METHONE

Encouraged by his successes of the previous two years beyond the Strymon and elsewhere, Philip too was able to take advantage of Athenian disillusionment, confident in his alliance with the Chalkidian cities. Very near to Emathia itself, between that plain and the conquered city of Pydna, lay Methone.[51] Any Macedonian communication between the heart of the kingdom and Pydna, the ancient towns of Dion and Herakleia in southern Pieria and, further south, Tempe and Thessaly must pass close by it or take the circuitous and difficult route through the mountains of the hinterland. Indeed it is difficult to understand how Philip had been able for so long to avoid facing the threat it posed; the answer must be sought partly in the seriousness of the succession of problems that had so far taken up his time and partly in the assumption that since 359, when they had played host to the Athenian force supporting Argaios, the people of Methone had lain low, relying ultimately on their fortifications to preserve them in case of attack. According to Diodoros[52] they were now permitting their city to become an enemy base, but he gives no indication of specific instances. However, the Athenians' decision ultimately, if too late, to send help to Methone suggests that they had hopes, possibly based on recent experience, of using it – and it guarantees that there was a substantial pro-Athenian group there. Further, that the siege of Methone drew Philip away from his campaigns against Athenian points in Thrace, to which he seems to have returned immediately afterwards, adds some strength to the supposition that the blockade was occasioned by a recent and specific instance of its danger to him.

In late 355 Macedonian forces were moved up to invest the city. Before the siege began Philip appears to have drawn up his forces near by and offered a delay during which the Methonaians might avert war by their surrender; in December honours were voted in Athens to one Lachares for his achievement in entering Methone,[53] which implies that the city was hard pressed but not yet under full siege. The length of the campaign, during which Philip lost his right eye to an arrow from the battlements, is unknown.[54] Athenian help was sent but arrived too late;[55] that it could be sent at all means that the spring (354) at least had arrived.[56] On their surrender the citizens were obliged to hand over their city and to depart, each with a single garment and no other possessions.[57] The walls and buildings were razed and the fertile land distributed among Macedonians.[58]

Meanwhile, during spring 354 Philomelos the Phokian had taken the offensive in central Greece, advancing into Lokris where he defeated in a cavalry engagement a combined force of Lokrians and Boiotians.[59] Six thousand 'Thessalians and their neighbouring allies',[60] presumably attempting to join forces with their Amphiktyonic colleagues, were cut off and defeated.[61] But the appearance in autumn of a large Boiotian force – the Amphiktyons now well outnumbering the Phokians, their mercenaries and allies, including new Peloponnesian reinforcements – forced Philomelos to a pitched battle at Neon in which his troops were badly defeated and he himself lost his life. His co-commander Onomarchos gathered up the survivors and led them back to Phokis.[62]

During these campaigns, probably early in their course, Methone fell. In what was apparently a related campaign another town, Pagai, which is otherwise unknown, was defeated and compelled to submit.[63]

ABDERA, MARONEIA AND NEAPOLIS

To Thrace Philip returned in summer or autumn 354, this time by sea, not to consolidate his hold on the western area but to press beyond the Nestos towards the wealthy coastal towns of Abdera and Maroneia, both, again, allies of Athens. Abdera, to judge by its tribute, had been the third wealthiest member of the Delian League and Maroneia was not far behind; both had acquired their wealth through trade with the Thracian hinterland. Typically for this area, these towns perched above the coast, the former on the bluff of Cape Baloustro, rising out of the marshy ground that extends eastward from the Nestos mouth and makes passage along or near the coast difficult or impossible, the latter on the stepped slopes of Mt Ismaros where it touches the shoreline at Cape Charalambos. The coast here and to the east where Mesymbria and Ainos lay was and is inhospitable, so that the most natural angle of attack was from the landward side; without control of the approaches this was however not possible for Philip without first moving his troops and equipment into the general area by sea. The date of this campaign is admittedly conjectural.[64] But Polyainos groups together the fall of Abdera with that of Maroneia, and Demosthenes refers (admittedly inconclusively) to Philip's having landed at the latter before 352; the date adopted here is the latest at which Philip is known to have been in Thrace before that time.[65] Maroneia and probably Abdera lay within the realm of King Amadokos of central Thrace, who in this his first known contact with Philip barred the Macedonian's way inland

and further east. It seems likely that the Thracian was acutely conscious of the danger to his own kingdom should the forces of Philip join those of his neighbour Kersebleptes, whose territory extended from the Hebros to the area of Perinthos and Byzantion.[66]

Philip was not prepared to press the issue. Neither of the two towns he had just taken was vital to any conceivable Macedonian expansionist interests in Thrace; the natural east-west route by-passed both by some distance inland. Their significance for him lay purely in their relationship with Athens. To have pushed onwards against Amadokos would have left him with a tenuous line of naval communication depending on a small fleet and, at the Thracian end, a poor harbour; by land he was isolated. In any case he achieved some agreement with Kersebleptes without actually making contact with him. Demosthenes refers to a pact arranged here, in which the Theban Pammenes played a role.[67] For, following the Amphiktyonic victory at Neon, the Thebans, in near fatal overconfidence but eager for the financial rewards,[68] despatched this general with 5000 troops to the aid of the Phrygian Artabazos in his continuing revolt against the Persian monarch (winter 354/3).[69] His assistance at Maroneia was no doubt rendered as the *xenos* of Philip.[70] The truth of his assertion the orator supports with a letter from the Athenian general Chares, which is not extant but the fact of which is useful to us in putting him in the area at the time. We may well doubt, indeed, since Chares was near by, whether it was alone the interdiction of Amadokos that deterred Philip from going beyond Maroneia.

The pact sealed, Philip re-embarked the infantry and assault equipment in his small fleet and sailed for home. But at Neapolis Chares was lying in ambush for him with 20 ships beached there at the ready, and only by drawing the Athenians' pursuit with his four fastest ships was Philip able to slip past with his transports.[71] The lesson, however, was not lost on him; the policy of eradicating potential Athenian bases without first securing the communication lines by land was dangerous. Neapolis itself, clearly, was at this time free of Macedonian control, whether because it had not yet been taken or (more likely) because, once taken, it was re-won by Chares. More pressing matters might require Philip's immediate attention, but some rationalization of Macedonia's eastward interests could not long be delayed.

PHERAI AND PHOKIS

Meanwhile another appeal had arrived from the Thessalian *koinon*, which again sought aid in its resistance to the depredations of

Lykophron at Pherai. In Philip's absence in Thrace the Amphiktyons' position in central Greece had deteriorated. At the end of winter, in early 353, Onomarchos, a capable successor to Philomelos, had seized upon the absence of Pammenes and his troops to redouble the Phokian efforts. In the spring he convened what was recorded as a meeting of the Amphiktyonic Council; those represented were Athens, Lokris, Megara, Epidauros, Sparta and Korinth, as well as the hosts, Phokis and Delphoi.[72] With the blessing of his allies, Onomarchos made good the losses suffered by the army at Neon and embarked on a series of successful campaigns against neighbouring Lokris, taking near-by Amphissa (which was vital for control of the northward mountain-route by-passing Thermopylai into Malis) and Thronion, one of the three strategic towns controlling the southern road to Thermopylai itself (the others being Nikaia and Alponos). Turning south through Dorian territory, which he ravaged, he moved then westwards into Boiotia, there taking Orchomenos. But his ensuing blockade of Chaironeia was unsuccessful and a defeat at Theban hands decided him to return to Phokis.[73] In any case he had been summoned, probably by this time, into Thessaly by his brother Phayllos.

The movements of Onomarchos during these few months had been the easier not only for the absence of Pammenes and his 5000 but also for the failure of the Thessalians to support their allies. This is explained by Diodoros as the result of Phokian bribes – and such may have been offered and received. But more essentially the reason was that by the summer of 353 Philip's Thessalian allies were again hard pressed by Pherai – and, to judge by the easy collusion that follows between the tyrant and his Phokian friends, the two sets of affairs were related.[74] During the summer, then, Philip returned to Thessaly where he again took up the league's cudgels.[75] On this occasion, probably for the first time (at least since 358) he entered the fray in person – most probably as the ally of Thebes as well as Thessaly[76] and possibly as the elected archon of the *koinon* (see below).

The initial campaigning against Lykophron, of which we know no details, evidently went well for the league, for the tyrant turned for relief to Phokis, whence Phayllos was despatched with aid. But on entering Thessaly he was met, defeated and driven back out of the country by the Macedonian king.[77] This reverse probably contributed to Onomarchos' decision to abandon his Boiotian campaign and he now moved his entire force to the north, apparently hoping that a substantial success now would give him control of the whole of Thessaly.[78] His army outnumbered that of his opponents and he had with him field artillery that would increase his advantage if he could deploy it effectively. When the Macedonian and Thessalian forces went to meet him he inflicted two defeats on them.[79] The military writer Polyainos[80] describes an effective stratagem employed by the Phokian that must relate to one of these battles: allowing Philip to advance towards him he concealed infantry and catapults on the slopes of a semicircular range of hills; then he drew up his remaining units at the entrance to the valley below, into which, when the attack came, the Phokian troops were to feign retreat. The ploy was successful. It may not have been practical for Philip to send out light horsemen to scout the slopes ahead of him. At any rate, when the enemy fled before him he pursued them, as planned, until those on the slopes declared their presence with bursts of stone-shot from their catapults into the massed ranks below. Macedonian casualties in the fusillade and the ensuing infantry charge were heavy and, although the king himself escaped unscathed, it was to face desertions among his battered, demoralized troops. With difficulty he reasserted control and, opting for discretion, retired to winter at home – withdrawing, as he claimed, 'like a ram to butt the harder next time'.

This is the only known occasion on which Philip's relations with his subjects were put under strain. Although Demosthenes[81] was to claim only three years after this that the Macedonian people were exhausted by Philip's ambitions and tired of the demands he made upon them, he was unable on any occasion to cite any single example of such dissatisfaction. Significantly, the only occasion on which Philip appears to have lost control, if temporarily, this lapse was brought about by a remarkable military error on his part – something of which he was rarely, if ever guilty otherwise. Disillusionment of course was not new to the Macedonians, but one can well imagine the effect of this defeat when, after six years of unmitigated military success, it must have appeared at first that their buoyant new balloon had burst.

Bitter was the pill. But it was not without its lessons for the king. He had perhaps underestimated the strength of his opponents, for it was the first time he had faced a large, efficient and well equipped mercenary force supported by the newly developed and costly artillery now available to those states with the wealth to pay for it.[82] In his account of the campaign of 353 Diodoros does not mention the Pheraian forces; neither do they appear in his account of the famous battle fought in the following year. At that time, on the Crocus Field, Onomarchos is said to have had 20,000 foot and 500 horse, and Philip slightly above that in infantry as well as 3000 cavalry. Since Onomarchos is also said to have brought his entire military strength in 353 his numbers were presumably similar then, whereas Philip and the Thessalians were numerically inferior. The Macedonian king was to demonstrate often in his career a notable economy in his military actions; he avoided fighting when this was possible and, when it was unavoidable, did not use unnecessarily high levies.[83] On the other hand, neither did he again use inadequate forces. The role of Philip in the development of Greek artillery was to be an important one and he had perhaps already begun developing such weapons in Macedonia. Arrow-shooting catapults were to play a part in the capture of Olynthos in 348 (bolt-heads some three to four inches long and stamped 'Philip's' were found in the excavations there) and were to attract attention in the siege of Perinthos in 340,[84] but it is quite likely that the real impetus for such development came from the setback suffered at the hands of Onomarchos in 353.[85]

THRACIAN REVERSES

In Thrace the Athenian general Chares was quick to profit from Philip's involvement. He had been unsuccessful, as we have seen, in his attempted naval ambush of Philip's fleet on its return from Maroneia. But when the Macedonian forces immediately marched south into Thessaly Chares perceived the vulnerability of Philip's Thracian arrangements and he now took the opportunity to upset them. In the late spring or early summer of 353 he sailed to the Chersonesos where he captured Sestos, slaying its male citizens and enslaving the rest.[86] Such savage treatment was not implemented without a purpose. The key to Athenian control of this peninsula was Kersebleptes, whose territory bordered it and whose claim to ownership of it at this time was backed by his derivation of an annual revenue of 30 talents from its towns. In spite of his agreement of 357 with Athens the Thracian had since that time continually worked against Athenian interests in the furtherance of his own ambitions to re-create his father's kingdom. In reaction, his associate kings Berisades (and then Ketriporis) and Amadokos had faithfully served Athens; most recently, in early 353, the latter had opposed Philip's eastward movement from Maroneia, but he had not been able to prevent his reaching some agreement with Kersebleptes' envoy Apollonides. The Athenians thus found themselves in the unsatisfactory position of supporting two kings in whom they were only marginally interested against the one whose co-operation they most vitally required. In this context Chares' capture and brutal treatment of the Sestians may be seen as a powerful attempt to force Kersebleptes into line. He, seeing Philip defeated by Onomarchos in the late summer or autumn, took the only path open to him and accepted Chares' terms. (That this would and did inevitably drive Ketriporis and Amadokos towards Philip was of secondary importance to Athens, whose concern now was to win over the rest of the Chersonesan towns and to maintain Kersebleptes' allegiance.)[87] He undertook to support Athenian attempts on Amphipolis and renounced his rights over the Chersonesan towns (except Kardia, at the narrow neck of the peninsula) and their tribute. The Athenians promptly sent cleruchs to Sestos and elsewhere.[88]

THE THREAT OF DISINTEGRATION

A second and very serious consequence of Philip's defeat in Thessaly was a similar willingness on the part of the Chalkidian League, or at least of its leading city, to seek accommodation with Athens. The Olynthians declared their friendship for the Athenians and stated their willingness to negotiate an alliance.[89] There was evidently a growing anti-Macedonian group at Olynthos, possibly, as Demosthenes says, alarmed at the growing power of Philip's Macedonia, and this no doubt played a part in the overtures. But two things suggest that this was not the main stimulus to a change of heart.[90] In the first place, the Olynthian offer appears to have been made around the time (and therefore quite possibly because) of Philip's loss in Thessaly; that is to say it appears to have been an attempt to placate an increasingly energetic enemy when the signs were that their strongest ally was about to collapse. Secondly, the lack of response from Athens (there being still no alliance at the time of Demosthenes' first two *Olynthiacs* four years later) suggests that, at least in the Athenians' assessment, the offer was a mere expedient indicating no real change of heart. As was to emerge over the next few years, the anti-Macedonian group at Olynthos was growing in power; but we are not warranted in assuming that they were yet dominant in late 353.

These are the only specifically attested instances of breakdown in Philip's relations with his neighbours and they by themselves were serious enough; but there is reason for suspecting that his problems went further than this. Indirect evidence suggests that in Epeiros and possibly also in Paionia and Illyria the existing settlements began to crumble.[91]

In central Greece early in the new year (352) Onomarchos acted. Seeing the importance for Philip of the coming months and realizing that the Macedonian would be desperate to bring their conflict to a successful conclusion, he launched a quick campaign into Boiotia to neutralize her in the impending struggle. He took Koroneia and possibly Korsiai and Tilphosaion.[92]

VICTORY IN THESSALY

When Philip returned to Thessaly in the spring of 352 he was conscious that much depended on the issue of that year. Sinking morale among his own people and defections among his allies demanded a definitive and spectacular success, and even then he would need to follow it up quickly to recover his position among the buffer areas. In Thessaly he again commanded combined forces of the league and Macedon, numbering now more than 20,000 foot and 3000 horse. Receiving intelligence of this Lykophron of Pherai no doubt again sent word to Onomarchos, who prepared to bring his forces north. The Athenians, persuaded by Phokian funds[93] to man their fleet, agreed to provide naval support, with the aim first of preventing the loss of Pagasai to Philip. Chares was sent into the Gulf of Pagasai.

The Macedonian preparations are significant. According to Justin,[94] Philip instructed his forces to wear crowns of laurel, 'as if he were avenging not the Thebans but an act of sacrilege, and went into battle as if led by the god'. Some have doubted whether Philip fought here as the ally of Thebes, but even if this, the only explicit evidence, is rejected, such preparations – in effect, the assumption of the cause of Apollo – as well as the events following the battle, again with the emphasis on the religious motive, make it clear that the Macedonian king wished to be seen defending his Thessalian allies and additionally acting in the wider Amphiktyonic role on behalf of those who had lost Apollo's city to the Phokian commanders.

The first action of the campaign was Philip's attack on Pagasai.[95] It was probably this, if not his very arrival, that prompted the Pheraian appeal to Phokis, but by the time the latter forces were through Thermopylai on their way to Pagasai the port had fallen into Philip's hands and the Macedonian army was able to meet the Phokians on the Krokion Plain[96] ('Crocus Field') where the cavalry could be used to advantage. Chares also arrived too late to help Pagasai and sailed down the western side of the gulf to give whatever assistance he could, but, with Pagasai lost, there was little open to him.

Thus in spring or early summer 352 the two armies met. Little information survives on the course of the battle except for the comment in Diodoros that Philip's dominance in cavalry was the decisive factor.[97] In the course of the Macedonian victory many Phokians fled to the beaches where Chares' fleet was cruising offshore, and stripping off their armour attempted to swim to the ships. Among these was Onomarchos, on whose death however the tradition is confused; most likely he was killed or drowned in this last phase of the battle and Philip afterwards hanged or crucified his body as befitted the despoiler of the temple.[98] Six thousand Phokians and their mercenaries had been killed in the fighting and the three thousand captured were then drowned as temple robbers.[99] Lykophron of Pherai, now friendless and hard pressed, offered his city to Philip under truce; the latter, realizing that the Sacred War was no more finished than it had been after the death of Philomelos at Neon and that the time was now ripe to carry the fighting into central Greece, accepted the offer and allowed the tyrant family and two thousand of their mercenaries to depart; they promptly joined Phayllos, the brother of Onomarchos and successor to his Phokian command.[100]

After the victory, probably during the late spring and early summer of 352, Philip remained in Thessaly. He had learnt from the previous year's troubles in the north and northeast the danger of transferring his efforts to a new front when unfinished business lay behind him. So that, even though an immediate dash in pursuit of the battered survivors of Crocus Field might have taken him through Thermopylai before Phayllos could call up support from his allies, he first began the task of securing Thessaly. In a speech delivered around May or June 341 (the third *Philippic*) Demosthenes would date the beginning of Philip's rise to power in the Greek world from a point 'thirteen incomplete years' before that time, evidently somewhere within the year 354/3 – and, whether or not we incline to agree with him, the orator's definition of the achievement that began Philip's rise is important as a contemporary assessment. But it is difficult to identify what he had in mind.[101] The fall of Methone, since its capture secured the coastal route to Thessaly and eliminated the last non-Macedonian enclave from Macedonian soil, might well represent a suitable achievement; but it probably belongs late in the year 355/4 rather than in 354/3 (though the latter is possible)[102] and in any case relates much more naturally to the question of Macedonian sovereignty than to the growth of its influence beyond its borders. The activities in Thrace later in 354/3 were hardly definitive – indeed from the Athenian point of view any gains there were substantially vitiated by the end of 353 as a result of Chares' actions. The most likely candidate then is the Thessalian intervention beginning in the summer of 353, although it was not until the following year that success attended it. Arguably the catalyst out of which Philip's rise to Greek dominance was formed, in Demosthenes' view, was the close relationship that inspired and, more importantly, grew from Philip's co-operation with the Thessalian League.

At some time during 353 or – if not then – in the following year, the League elected Philip its archon, or *tagos*.[103] This was a constitutionally defined office, lifelong in tenure and presumably military, or largely so, in function – though the *auctoritas* of the appointee will in practice have given him wider influence over the league's affairs. What was unprecedented and altogether remarkable was its conferment on a foreigner. We can hardly be satisfied with the negative justification advanced by Justin;[104] Philip must have shown himself convincingly a friend of the league and an assiduous protector of its interests in the years between his accession and 353. The proceeds of the Thessalian harbour and market dues, again either before or in 352, were granted to the new archon, perhaps as a normal accompaniment to the office – though possibly as a separate act, since an assembly of the league could allegedly contemplate at a later date the withdrawal of these revenues from the archon's control.[105] The purpose of the grant was clearly to finance what military schemes the commander-in-chief was called upon or decided to perform – although Demosthenes, very likely out of ignorance, was to put it more broadly: 'the Thessalian League should be administered from these revenues and they should not go into Philip's own pocket'.[106] Together with this grant went the cession of Thessaly's main harbour, Pagasai, controlled for the previous 50 years by the tyrant house at near-by Pherai. It is an excellent port, the only one to speak of on the Thessalian coastline (it lies very near modern Volos) and its acquisition by Philip is probably to be interpreted partly in financial terms (since it will have been the main – virtually the only – source of harbour dues) and partly with the intention of preventing Athenian interference in Thessaly – rather than with a view to its offensive naval use on any scale. It is likely, however, that the occasional small raids made southwards to the Athenian area by Philip's small fleet will have been launched from here. By the end of 351 he had made at least two such sorties, one to Geraistos where, so Demosthenes claimed, he seized the Athenian merchant fleet and one a landing at Marathon where he captured the Paralos, one of Athens' sacred triremes.[107] With Pagasai for a base surprise attacks would be the more effective, escape from superior fleets quicker and easier and the perils of open-sea sailing might be largely avoided.

The cession of Pagasai was made at the expense of Pherai but Philip's settlement with the latter city was in the main directed at winning friendships, not prolonging enmities. After the departure of the tyrants and their mercenaries he organized a personal settlement with the inhabitants. He married a woman of Pherai, Nikesipolis, whose daughter, in recognition of the victory of 352, was to be named Thessalonike.[108] This marriage we must take as a sign that Philip wished to draw a distinction in his treatment of the Pheraians between the tyrants and their adherents on the one hand and their innocent subjects on the other

– a policy he was to attempt to repeat six years later in Phokis, but in that case without success. In Pherai, if he hoped by adopting this line to make of the people his reliable supporters, he was however to be disillusioned before long. Whether this settlement was ordained by the king of the Macedonians or by the archon of the Thessalian League we cannot tell; if Nikesipolis became his wife on the same terms as her predecessors and successors then the former is implied. In general terms we may only say that he should have conducted his negotiations in the same *persona* as that in which he had defeated the tyrants; but since that is unknown and was at least ambiguous (encompassing the roles certainly of foreign ally and possibly of Thessalian archon) the question cannot be answered.

When we discover what other territories were ceded to the Macedonian we begin to understand his immediate interest in Thessaly. He was already the ally of the league in a much more intimate sense than the usual, but he now began in addition to acquire control in the *perioikis*, the three neighbouring areas of Perrhaibia, Magnesia and Achaia-Phthiotis, all of which were of strategic value and all of which exercised votes in the Amphiktyonic Council. He now obtained at least parts of the first two of these territories.

Magnesia, to which Pagasai had once belonged and was now technically restored in accordance with Philip's promise,[108a] comprised for the most part the long range of mountains running north and south between the Thessalian plain and the Aegean coast, from the Pass of Tempe in the north to the far tip of the western arm of the Pagasitic Gulf; indeed Magnesia is little more than its mountains, Ossa and Pelion together with the lower Mavrovouni (its modern name) between them. Its coastline is difficult of access and contains no usable harbours. However, since Philip is said to have made plans to fortify some of its towns[109] it is evident that it must have been a more significant area than its topography might suggest; possibly he was interested mainly in its extreme north, where it terminates at Tempe, and at its extreme south, on the gulf.

The strategic importance of Perrhaibia is immediately plain. It controlled both means of southern access to Macedonia, either along the Peneios through Tempe or northwards to Oloosson (modern Elassona) and thence behind Olympos and through the mountain-passes into Elimeia. The Perrhaibians, although in theory autonomous (they, like the Magnesians, exercised two Amphiktyonic votes at Delphi), had in reality been subject to Larisa. Their tribute to the latter was now remitted instead to Philip.[110] This cession of the northern part of Perrhaibia[111] may be seen as a gesture of goodwill and gratitude on the part of the league or of its dominant city; as Philip had acted generously in devoting time and effort to the safeguarding of Thessalian security so the league now reciprocated in kind and to the same end.[112]

Perrhaibia, like Magnesia, was garrisoned and fortified at certain points. Gonnoi, the key to Tempe,[113] became in effect a colony, whose defence and administration were Macedonian-organized and whose population was heavily Macedonian in content – in the same way and for the same reasons as had Philippoi four years earlier.[114] No doubt Oloosson too received at least a garrison.

It may also have been in 353 or 352 that Philip intervened in a war being fought between the Hestiaiotian towns of Pelinna and Pharkadon. He captured and destroyed the latter and possibly near-by Trikka as well,[115] leaving Pelinna and Gomphoi dominant in the region, an area that again was important for its access to Epeiros, Athamania and Ambrakia. Gomphoi in particular seems to have been elevated from obscurity by Macedonian colonization under the name Philippoi or Philippopolis.[116] When these actions took place we cannot be absolutely certain – whether, for example, they were completed before Philip's departure from Thessaly or (more plausibly) were merely by then planned for later execution. The reasonable assumption though is that they were the actions of the archon following concessions by a grateful league. At any rate, when Philip withdrew from Thessaly in the middle of the year, his settlement there was to remain secure for some three years before any signs of strain showed, and these were to be removed quickly and with little apparent difficulty.

THERMOPYLAI

First, however, having secured his position there, the king turned to the task of pursuing the Phokians through Thermopylai. But Phayllos had not been idle in the months since his brother's death at Crocus Field. Turning again to the sacred treasures of Delphi he coined large amounts of silver and gold, prepared a large arsenal and attracted additional mercenaries with inflated wages. Three of his allies, the Achaians, Spartans and Athenians, supported him with forces and to these he was able to add the Pheraian exiles.[117] When Philip reached the northwestern entrance to the pass he was confronted by a large army comprising all these elements; for allies he had none but the Thessalians and he would certainly require help from the southern end of the narrow pass between cliffs and sea. This might have come from the Thebans and the Boiotian League, but so effective had been the precautions taken by Onomarchos between his Thessalian campaigns of

353 and 352 that these, finding the large enemy force[118] in control of Thermopylai and its approaches and with Phokian sympathizers holding Orchomenos, Koroneia and by now probably Korsiai and Tilphosaion, were not prepared to risk an attack on Phayllos' rear. Rather than waste time and men on a protracted assault or on a wearing march by the difficult alternative route through Doris, Philip retired, frustrated again by the now dead Onomarchos.

THE THRACIAN CAMPAIGN OF 352/351

But it was perhaps as well. Thracian affairs had gone unattended for too long and it was in this direction that Philip now turned his attention. Leaving Thermopylai around the middle of the summer and presumably picking up replacements and equipment en route at Pella, the Macedonian army by November of the same year was at Heraion, nearly 700 km. distant on the Propontine coast in close proximity to Perinthos.

When they had left Thrace only eighteen months before, in the spring of 353, it had been at the end of a successful (though hardly conclusive) campaign. In the interim, as we have seen, the skill of the Athenian Chares had wrought a drastic change for the worse.[119] The Chersonesos was now again Athenian, with her cleruchs firmly in control. Kersebleptes, forced to foreswear his short-lived Macedonian attachment,[120] had returned to his old policy of reconstructing his father's dismembered kingdom, now with the tacit approval of the Athenians. Philip, on his return, found the Thracian under attack over disputed territory from three of his disgruntled neighbours, the Byzantines, Perinthians and Amadokos, king of central Thrace.[121] His offer of assistance was accepted and it was as their ally that Philip invested the Heraion fortress. News travelled quickly to Athens. Confident from their recent gains in this area and at the general weakening of Philip's hold on the areas to his east, the assembly now saw its opportunity to defeat a foe fighting among his enemies and far from home. In a noisy assembly a force of 40 triremes was proposed and approved and arrangements made to call a levy of all those up to 45 years of age and to impose an *eisphora* to raise 60 talents.[122] But, probably very soon afterwards, there were second thoughts. For one thing, Kersebleptes was too undependable to entrust to his loyalty a substantial part of the male citizenry. More importantly, however, it was soon learnt that Philip was far from alone in this campaign, that he was acting in concert with three allies, at least one of which, Byzantion, had an impressive fleet. The excitement died and the expedition lapsed with it, before even reaching the water. All that was left for the Athenians was to await developments.

In Thrace the siege continued, while Philip, in addition, took measures to ensure for himself a degree of influence in Thracian internal matters – probably in eastern Thrace and with the support of his new ally Amadokos. He removed some local leaders from their positions and replaced them with others of his own choosing.[123] The year (352/1) passed with no further developments until, perhaps in July or August, rumours began reaching Athens to the effect that Philip was ill or even dead;[124] the former, it was to turn out, was the truth. To the Athenians it now seemed that the enemies of Kersebleptes might withdraw their forces from their dangerous proximity to the Chersonesos.[125] A small fleet was contemplated and, possibly at this point, established; it might be despatched from the city, once the fighting was known to have ceased, with the task of reconnoitring the effects of the campaign on Athenian interests. In September it set out. In the meantime Philip, recovered from his illness and with Heraion taken and handed back to its original owner (presumably Perinthos), began the march back to Pella.[126]

However, further unfinished business awaited him, in the Chalkidike, Epeiros and possibly Paionia and Illyria,[127] and he detoured into the territory of the first of these. As we have seen, the Olynthians at least, during his absence in Thessaly and probably at the time of his setback there in the 353 campaign, had in principle forsworn their agreement with him and were even seeking alliance with his Athenian enemy.[128] What action he now took is unclear. Although Demosthenes implies some sort of military venture his precise meaning is indistinct ('... he "made an attempt on" the Olynthians'). Theopompos, in what is apparently a reference to the same incident, has Philip (by implication at least) delivering a stern warning to the leaders of the Chalkidians.[129] It is impossible to choose between, on the one hand, an ambiguity and, on the other, a far from complete and certainly inexplicit piece of information; what does emerge is that Philip was not yet ready to seek a firm resolution of his relationship with this league. Very likely he recognized that a major factor in Olynthos' defection must have been its fear in 353 that the power of its ally was on the wane at the same time as its enemy, Athens, was recovering ground in the Thracian area; and this was a situation which was already beginning to improve. But, equally clearly, there was an influential anti-Macedonian faction at Olynthos, and to allow such a group unfettered freedom to oppose his interests was to invite trouble from a dangerous quarter. In 357 he had been prepared, with Athens weakened by war with her own allies, to surrender his alliance with her in exchange for one with his powerful neighbour. But now, in 351, although Athens was still relatively weak, her northern ambitions and interests were reviving, and this, combined with the rising influence of his enemies in the Chalkidike, augured ill for the future of his arrangements. The time had arrived for a reconsideration of the basis of Macedonian policy.

CHAPTER IV

351–346
TOWARDS A GREEK SETTLEMENT

KING ARYBBAS OF EPEIROS

BELIEVING THAT HE HAD SETTLED the Chalkidian problem, at least for the time being, Philip turned to the reconstruction necessary on and beyond his northwestern and western frontiers. Some indications have already been noted that repercussions of the Macedonian setback of 353 had been felt in these areas also, and it is probably now, after his campaigns in the east and south of the kingdom, that Philip began to attend to difficulties with Illyrian and Paionian tribes and with King Arybbas of Epeiros. Of a Paionian campaign we know no detail, but it may be the action that led Isokrates to remark four years later that Philip had made subjects of them. Probably, from this time, Lyppeios (and later Patraos, who succeeded him, apparently in the late 330s)[1] paid a tribute to the Macedonian king and was liable to supply troops at his request.

In the same passage, Isokrates implies that a Macedonian expedition (probably in 351/0) was successful in establishing control over areas rendered unstable by the great Dardanian defeat of 358; one example of the same instability had already presented itself in the movement of the Grabaioi from the distant northwest to the very frontiers of the kingdom.[2] So far as we can tell, the Illyrian and Paionian campaigns were consistent with the general strategy Philip had adopted in dealing with these neighbours: one of pacification, where necessary reinforced by periodic demonstrations of Macedonian superiority. No Macedonian governors or military commanders appear to have been assigned to these areas, and, to our knowledge, there was no interference with their local government or organization. They were regarded as client-areas.

With Epeiros, on the other hand, the king was concerned to build a solid relationship that might guarantee him firm protection on his southwestern flank, as well as control over the alternative north/south passage, which ran from the northwestern Peloponnesos, across the Straits of Rhion, through Aitolia and Ambrakia to Epeiros. Some seven years earlier his marriage with Olympias, niece (and sister-in-law) of the reigning AryBbas, had had this end in view; its first product, Alexander, was now six years old. No more than twelve years of age was his namesake, the younger brother of Olympias, at present living in the Molossian court of Epeiros. In 350, war broke out between the two kingdoms – perhaps because Arybbas too had not hidden his disquiet over Philip's reverse of 353 and had sought support elsewhere; or perhaps simply because Philip had designs on certain Epeirote territory in the region of the Pindos range near the common frontier of the two states. Of the course of this struggle we know nothing, but of its issue some features are clear. The young Alexandros was removed from his uncle's court and taken to Pella, where Philip would arrange for his education and training until he was ready to instal him on the throne that had been his father's. This may have been inspired in part by Olympias, who must, like Philip, have recognized that the danger to her brother's life increased as he grew nearer the age at which he might occupy the throne. But, equally important, Philip had decided to bind the neighbouring kingdom to himself more closely than was possible with Arybbas on the throne.[3]

So it was that the status of King Arybbas underwent a change at the end of this campaign. Although, at the death of his predecessor, Neoptolemos, the latter's son would normally have inherited the throne, Alexandros was very young, and – his situation apparently being closely analogous to that of the young Amyntas on the death of Perdikkas III of Macedon – was evidently passed over for his uncle, whom our sources appear unanimously to regard as king. It seems likely that, as a complement to his plans to plant his brother-in-law on the Molossian throne, Philip at the same time forced Arybbas to regard himself for the time being as the boy's regent.[4] It was probably at this time that Tymphaia, Atintania and Paravaia were severed from Epeiros and annexed to the Macedonian kingdom; their addition completed Philip's hold on the Pindos range where it delimits the southwestern corner of Macedonia.[5]

If the dating of these three ventures – in Paionia, Illyria and Epeiros – is correct, then they will presumably have engaged Philip's attention through most of the year 350 and possibly in early 349. At any rate, nothing is known of other activities during that time.

ASIAN HORIZONS

When the Theban Pammenes had gone with 5000 infantry to Phrygia in early 353 to assist Artabazos in his revolt against the Great King, his success had been noteworthy, but he had then been dismissed by the satrap on suspicion of having plotted secretly with the king or his supporters. The loss of the Theban hoplite stiffening was fatal to the rebel cause and it collapsed soon afterwards. The satrap and his brother-in-law, the Rhodian Memnon, fled from the Persian domains (probably in late 353 or early 352) and successfully sought refuge at Pella.[6] There, for more than ten years, until their pardon and recall on the representations of Memnon's brother, Mentor, they and other refugees from the Persian yoke no doubt pressed for Philip's support against their erstwhile master. At some time before 346, and probably before his Chalkidian campaign began in 349, Philip seems to have decided to acquiesce in their wishes. There were many advantages to such plans. Ample wealth, especially by Greek standards, was to be found in Asia Minor, both in the Persian treasury at Sardis and in the tribute currently paid to the Persian realm, as well as in what booty might be won in the course of securing them. If he wished to win high prestige among the mainland Greeks, then he could do so by pushing the Persians out of the Greek-inhabited coastal satrapies of Asia Minor or out of Anatolia altogether. Perhaps more important, he was well aware of the political effects of the powerful military society he had built. Now, as never before, the bulk of Macedonian citizens must have had a heavy stake in military expansion. In military campaigning lay the *raison d'être* of the army – just as it provided the opportunities for the advancement and enrichment of its members. In Asia Minor suitable military goals might be found, which, for the indefinite future, offered fame and wealth as well as a means of absorbing the energies of his kingdom.

This idea now began to germinate. In the years that followed, as the impending break-down of relations with the Chalkidian cities became a reality, and as the king turned to a new alignment with the Athenians (those who had the greatest interest – an economic one – in the reopening of Asia Minor and its offshore islands to their trade), it seems to have governed his overall policy. Between 348 and 346 he would attempt to create a settlement of Greek affairs that would give him the co-operation of the Athenians in his venture and the stability of the Greek mainland behind his back.

PHOKIS AND PHERAI

Since the summer of 352, in Central Greece, Phokian fortunes under the new commander, Phayllos (and, after his death, Phalaikos, the son of Onomarchos) were very mixed. Although there were occasional successes on both sides, neither the Boiotian nor the Phokian forces were strong enough to bring an end to the Sacred War. The Phokians' policy continued in the cultivation of their allies, but, faced with an Athenian unwillingness to spend money on this war, they turned increasingly to their Peloponnesian friends, Sparta and Korinth, as well as other anti-Theban states, such as Epidauros, Phleios and perhaps others.[7] When war had broken out during 352/1 between Sparta and the Arkadians of Megalopolis (the allies of Thebes), the Phokians were quick to send 3000 infantry, who were accompanied by forces of the exiled Pheraian tyrants. In Athens, Demosthenes urged his fellows to add their support to Megalopolis, but to no avail. Returning successful from this campaign, a 4500-strong Boiotian army was able to eject Phalaikos from Chaironeia and to follow this with the devastation of much enemy territory. The exhaustion of the Phokians is reflected in their failure to continue the pretence of convening the rebel Amphiktyony after the spring meeting of 351; on the other hand, the Thebans, although readily furnished with cash by Artaxerxes Ochos, were unable to follow up their victory with more than minor skirmishes with their enemy.[8] The war had reached a stalemate, dragging through a series of desultory and indecisive engagements over the following years and resulting, in the early summer of 347, in the deposition of the hapless Phalaikos and, in reaction to the Phokian successes that ensued, a Theban appeal for Macedonian intervention.[9]

THE CHALKIDIAN CAMPAIGN

Meanwhile, by the middle of 349 events were moving in such a way as to bring Philip's Thessalian settlement under pressure. We know that mercenaries of the expelled Pheraian tyrants, Lykophron and Peitholaos, served in 351 on the Spartan side against the Arkadians and Thebans. The exiles had far from despaired of returning to their city and, perhaps at about the time that Philip began to move towards the Chalkidike, they were successful. Within a few months, Philip was to be obliged to give attention to Pherai, since it was thence, or from its port, Pagasai, that his major Thessalian revenues were derived.[10]

Precisely what brought the Macedonians and Chalkidians into conflict is not entirely clear. Perhaps, as most have thought, Philip had simply reached the stage at which he was ready to snatch this wealthy area for himself. But there may have been more to it. Soon after the warning issued to the Chalkidians in late 351 (possibly even immediately afterwards), the anti-Macedonian leader in Olynthos, one Apollonides, was banished. To the office of hipparch two pro-Macedonians were elected: Lasthenes and Euthykrates.[11] Demosthenes, who supplies the evidence for the expulsion, makes no mention of any direct (*i.e.*

military) pressure on Philip's part, but simply asserts that this was effected by Olynthians 'totally subservient to him', his partisans. Whatever the truth behind it, one thing is clear: that at that time Philip – if he was involved even indirectly – still hoped for a political solution to the problem of Chalkidian realignment. That this hope was vain is shown by the immediate pretext for the war eventually fought between the two states. Just before Olynthos was attacked in 348 (or before the general Chalkidian campaign began in autumn 349), Philip demanded that the Olynthians hand over to him two of his stepbrothers who were being harboured by the city. The inhabitants' refusal to do so was, according to one source, the cause of the war.[12]

There appear, at Philip's accession, to have been three members of this family: Archelaos, Menelaos and Aridaios, all older than the king himself, sons of his father by an earlier marriage.[13] Evidently, following the death of one of them, probably Archelaos, the two remaining brothers sought and found refuge in Olynthos. Since they are unlikely to have been given asylum before $c.350$ (for, if they had, they would surely have been expelled at the same time as Apollonides), it is justifiable to assume that in the last year before the Macedonian campaign against the Chalkidian cities there had been further signs of rift between the allies. By granting refuge and protection the Olynthians, presumably, were not acting out of humanitarian motives. In seeking an explanation our eye is inevitably drawn to the situation in the mid-380s, when Olynthos had installed Argaios as rival to the crown of Amyntas III. Presumably, in 350/49, this city had again evolved plans for advancing the claims of a pretender. Such a threat may well have given rise to the warning Philip is said to have delivered to his enemies as he advanced on their city. One of two things must happen: either they, the Olynthians, must abandon Olynthos, or he Macedonia [14] He appears to have grasped (what he failed to understand in 351/0) that the policies of Apollonides had been no temporary vacillation on his ally's part but were symptomatic of a revival of Olynthian ambitions, relatively dormant since 379. There was no room at close quarters for two such powers.

In early autumn of 349 he marched his forces across the frontier near Lake Bolbe and laid siege to the northeastern town of Stageira.[15] Occupying an important position quite close to the route (which ran north of the lake) between central Macedonia and Amphipolis, and, more importantly, commanding the best access from the eastern coastline to central and western Chalkidike, its fate was to sound a warning to the other communities of the peninsula. When it capitulated it was razed to the ground. Further towns, probably in the same area (certainly Stratonikeia and most likely Akanthos, Arethousa and perhaps even Apollonia),[16] capitulated without battle; Philip might now prevent the movement of enemy troops eastward towards Olynthos from the Strymonic Gulf coastline.

As soon as Macedonian intentions had become clear, Olynthian envoys travelled to Athens, renewing their past avowals of peace and goodwill and now asking urgently for alliance.[17] Their reception was not as they might have hoped. How much sympathy for their cause already existed among the Athenians we cannot be sure, but Demosthenes, for one, was prompted to deliver two separate speeches in their support and in both clearly implied that the opposition against which he argued was strong. In the second he professes himself puzzled that his fellows do not make an immediate decision and back it up forthwith by mounting an expedition.[18] Eventually, swallowing their suspicion of the petitioners and willing to see Philip thwarted, provided it was not substantially at their own cost, the assembly voted for alliance. The debate continued. Professions of alliance were no substitute for military aid and it was not very long before Demosthenes again rose to deliver the third of his speeches on the subject, urging the despatch of immediate and effective help in accordance with the new obligation. As a result – of the deliberations and not necessarily of this speech – a small force was detailed, comprising 30 ships (probably those on regular station in the north) with 2000 peltast mercenaries and an additional eight ships, the last apparently being launched as the result of an appeal for voluntary trierarchs.[19] Nothing is known of the activities of this force in the Chalkidike – very probably because no actual fighting was in progress at the time.

DISTRACTIONS IN THESSALY AND EUBOIA

It may have been that Philip wished to let the lesson of Stageira sink in before pressing eastwards against the more powerful members of the Chalkidian League. But, more certainly, he was forced to give attention to serious trouble in Thessaly. In the first of his speeches on Olynthos, Demosthenes had stated that 'the Thessalians' had voted to demand restoration of Pagasai and 'to make representations over Magnesia'.[20] In the second, delivered perhaps only days later, he had again alluded to the demand over Pagasai, noted that 'the Thessalians' had actually prevented Philip from fortifying Magnesia. He then produced a new datum recently come to his notice, that the revenues granted to the archon from harbour and market dues were to be cut off, since they were being spent on Macedonian and not Thessalian interests.[21] What appears to have transpired is that there had been a revival of Pheraian power under Peitholaos, which, combined (perhaps)[22] with dissatisfaction among other Thessalians over Philip's continuing failure to carry out his promises regarding the Phokian war, successfully produced a series of votes by the Thessalian *koinon* in favour of withdrawing his privileges – though not, it seems, of removing him from office. However, it is worth noting that the actions represented here by the orator as arising from the grievances of the Thessalian League accord closely with the inevitable effects of a *Pheraian* resurgence. Both Pagasai and Magnesia had been under Pheraian control until 352 and would have been among the first areas to fall under the control of the revived tyranny. Since Pagasai must have been a major source of at least the archon's customs dues, its seizure by Peitholaos would by itself remove a portion of this revenue from Philip's control. It is possible, that is, since we know independently of an intervention by Philip against Pherai at this time,[23] that Demosthenes, in order to lend courage to his fellows to challenge Philip in the north, was manufacturing a rift with the Thessalian League out of local difficulties in the region of Pherai.

By the time he came to deliver the third *Olynthiac* Demosthenes had nothing to say about affairs in Thessaly. Perhaps this was because he was concerned in that speech with the Athenian contribution to the defence of Olynthos, but it nevertheless implies (since the recent situation, if as serious as he had painted it, would have seriously affected Philip's ability to fight effectively) that the difficulty had been resolved in the interim. It is unlikely that Philip travelled in person to Thessaly; had he appeared so close to central Greece we should expect to hear of it. More probably, troops remaining nearby (at Gonnoi or elsewhere in northern Magnesia or in Perrhaibia) were detailed to perform the task, possibly with Thessalian assistance, while Philip and his main force prepared to resume the Chalkidian campaign during the next spring.

But, as Philip had to contend with his distractions, so, at the end of the winter, did the Athenian people – their decision to commit troops to Euboia, while diplomatically disastrous, serving to indicate to friend and enemy alike the main line of current Athenian policy. In 357 it had been clear, when their forces easily expelled a powerful Theban force from the island, that the key to influence over the Euboians was majority support among the islanders.[24] But this was a lesson the Athenians were quick to forget. By 349, Eretria lay under the hand of the tyrant Ploutarchos and his mercenaries, clearly with at least tacit Athenian approval. But when the tyrant, faced with internal revolt, appealed for aid, at which point the Athenians should have reconsidered their stance, they were persuaded to send a small force under Phokion, expecting (on what grounds remains incomprehensible, but presumably the assurance of Ploutarchos combined with blissful memories of the episode of 357) general support on the island. Phokion quickly realized the error and, fighting his way out of a tight corner, did his best to retrieve the situation;[25] but, in spite of the circumstances there, which evidently remained grim, he was recalled on other business.[26] On his departure the situation deteriorated disastrously, the Athenians were defeated, their relief commander captured and the *demos* was obliged to accept a few months later a settlement involving a large ransom and guaranteeing the independence of the Euboians. Only Karystos, on the southern tip of the island, retained its alliance with Athens.[27]

The affair obviously had been a serious miscalculation, but the motive behind it illustrates equally clearly what it was that might stir to action the *demos* that took such hesitant and half-hearted measures with regard to Olynthos. The Athenian people felt their primary loyalty to lie in protecting their immediate interests rather than in committing themselves to more distant (and therefore expensive) campaigns. The outcome of the Social War had produced this attitude; then the influence and conservative legislation of Euboulos had elevated it into policy.[28]

The converse is seen in the disparity between what aid Demosthenes urged must be given to the Olythians and the expeditions the Athenian *demos* actually sent. But, in any case, we must beware of elevating Demosthenes so early as this into a leading Athenian statesman – as also of believing his fellow citizens so gullible as to commit substantial forces to a distant zone in support of an ally whose bona fides was at least suspect, on the basis of past actions, and might evaporate at any time if Philip should offer sufficient inducement. It was at about this time that Aristotle, the man destined to be Stageira's greatest son and Plato's greatest pupil, left Athens and emigrated to the territory of the tyrant Hermias. Hermias, ex-slave and *castrato* by repute (but perhaps only out of the mouths of his enemies), had succeeded during the years of Persian impotence in Asia Minor in carving out for himself a thriving little princedom among the mountain-villages of the Troad and around the coastline opposite Lesbos between his seat of Atarneus and Assos. Wealthy and well furnished with mercenaries, he was recognized by a preoccupied Persia. With the Platonists Erastos and Koriskos from near-by Skepsis he formed with Plato's blessing a curious *amicitia*, establishing them as his 'companions' and advisers in Assos; their influence is said to have mellowed his rule.[29] Aristotle joined the 'companions' at Assos, where he passed three years combining study, teaching and political counselling in congenial company.

But there was more to it than this. Although it is impossible to sift facts from propaganda, there is not much doubt that Aristotle was no mere itinerant scholar and teacher. He was son of the Stageirite Nikomachos, who several decades earlier had been personal physician to Amyntas III, Philip's father. It is said that his departure from Athens (he had arrived there in 367) was occasioned by the death of Plato and the elevation of Speusippos, but he was also perhaps associated with Philip too closely for comfort in a city seething with news and rumour from the Chalkidike.[30] Travelling to Atarneus apparently by way of Macedonia he probably negotiated at this time an entente between Philip and Hermias, both of whom saw profit in an arrangement that promised for the former an Anatolian bridgehead and for the latter a stronger guarantee of independence from the clutches of Artaxerxes Ochos. With this preliminary step taken, Philip was now ready to set in train his plans for a Greek settlement which would allow him to turn with his new ally and an enthusiastic army towards the much greener pastures across the Aegean.[31]

THE FALL OF OLYNTHOS

In about March 348 he had returned to the attack in the Chalkidike, beginning a drive down the peninsula west of Olynthos to the areas of Bottiaia and Pallene (the westernmost peninsula), at least some major communities (perhaps all) submitting to him without battle.[32] A second Olynthian appeal to the Athenians elicited a response similar to the first. Charidemos, the general holding the regular command at the Hellespont, was ordered to Olynthos with 18 triremes (probably the ten he had taken in late 351,[33] augmented by the eight volunteers raised for the previous Olynthian expedition), 4000 peltast mercenaries and 150 horse.[34] Olynthos at this time (between March and May) was not yet under attack, for the Olynthians were able to combine with Charidemos in destructive raids in the areas recently fallen into Philip's hands.[35] How effective these were we do not know, but what was decisive – in late spring or early summer – was the capitulation to the Macedonian King of Mekyberna (the port of Olynthos) and Torone, by holding which Philip was able to cut off the Olynthians from the sea. The defenders brought up their forces but were defeated in two battles and confined to their walls. Under siege, they despatched, around the middle of the year, a third, desperate appeal for Athenian assistance further to what was there already.[36] From Athens 17 triremes, with 2000 hoplites and 300 cavalry in transport, set sail for the north under Chares' command.[37]

But Philip had timed his campaign well and bad weather (perhaps the northerly Etesian winds) hampered the contingent's voyage; it was not to reach Olynthos until after the city had fallen.[38] In fact, at about the time of its departure, quite possibly even before it had sailed, news was received in Athens that was calculated to cause confusion. A group of Euboian envoys, come to discuss terms relating to the recent Athenian campaign on the island,[39] brought the tidings that Philip no longer wished to be at war with the Athenians. This was only the first of a number of Macedonian overtures, which led eventually to the Peace of Philokrates. But the timing of this initiative, at about the time of the investment of the city of Olynthos itself, was probably designed to weaken the Athenian will to assist its ally. The reaction of the *demos* is not recorded, but it was probably unfavourable; the majority, like Demosthenes, had committed itself (however half-heartedly) to the northern alliance and was not interested in peace.[40]

Before very long – probably in August or September – the Olynthian siege was over. Philip's partisans in the beleaguered city played their role. Two of them, the hipparchs Lasthenes and Euthykrates, surrendered 500 cavalry to him and soon afterwards the city fell.[41] After plundering it and enslaving the inhabitants, says Diodoros, he sold everything as booty. The Olynthians themselves were in fact probably treated according to their political alignments, although most of our sources appear to believe that all suffered the same fate.[42] Chalkidian territory (or some of it) was allotted to Macedonians – at least to members of the *hetairos*-class, who appear later in Alexander's cavalry as the squadrons from Apollonia and Anthemous.[43] Athenian citizens captured during the campaign were transported to Pella and held there; Philip had other plans for them. In Athens itself, the Assembly could do no more than grant refuge and citizenship to the Olynthians who had escaped, pass condemnatory motions against their betrayers and engage in recriminations against their own generals.[44]

PEACE-MOVES

Such a brave show however could not hide the gloomy prospect facing the city. When news of Philip's unqualified victory was received they knew too that, with the allies of Thebes disillusioned by their failure to finish off an equally depressed Phokis, it was only a matter of time before the victor at Olynthos was invited into central Greece. Then, as the ally of the Phokians and the enemy of Thebes, Athens was in grave danger of direct attack. It was therefore with a sense of relief and jubilation that the Athenians received a second message from Philip, sent to capitalize upon their depression.

Shortly before the fall of Olynthos, during the Olympic truce of 348 (so probably in July) an Athenian, Phrynon of Rhamnous, had been captured by pirates who were apparently Macedonian or at least operating out of some part of the Macedonian realm. When he had arranged his own ransom, Phrynon presented himself before the *demos*, requesting the despatch to Philip of an official envoy to complain of this violation of the sacred truce and to ask recompense of his costs. Ktesiphon was sent, returning – by now certainly after the fall of Olynthos – with news of Philip's goodwill towards the Athenians and his assurance that, having entered the war with them in the first place against his wishes, he was eager even after his recent success to be quit of it. Although they may have doubted his avowals, they eagerly received Ktesiphon's report and conferred upon him an official vote of praise.[45] Philokrates, demesman of Hagnous and associate of Demosthenes,[46] rose to move that Philip be invited to send envoys to discuss terms; the assembly affirmed the proposal to a man.[47] The motion, however popular, was technically illegal, probably because a clause in the Athenian/Olynthian alliance will have forbidden any negotiations with the enemy by either party without the prior assent of the other.[48] When the case came to trial Demosthenes spoke in Philokrates' defence and won such an overwhelming victory that the plaintiff was fined and lost his right in the future to prosecute such a suit.[49]

THE DECREE OF EUBOULOS

While it is clear that the immediate reaction of most Athenians to the signs that Philip would not immediately march south with his Thessalian and Boiotian allies to crush all who stood against him was one of relief and even pleasure, it is equally clear that Philip had as yet no cause for complacency. While the Athenian people were happy to play the jade to Philip's advances, they were equally prepared to see what resistance could be organized among the Greek states to crush him, or at least to defend Thermopylai against him. Within a short time of the fall of Olynthos, Euboulos persuaded the very *demos* that had recently welcomed Philip's friendliness to despatch a number of embassies to the Greek states – 'almost as far as the Red Sea', as Demosthenes ironically remarked[50] – with a view to inviting them to make war in common against Philip. It was Euboulos' decree, but he had been greatly assisted in its passage by the appearance of his younger colleague, the actor Aischines, who dramatically introduced Ischandros the Arkadian as 'the representative of the friends of Athens in Arkadia'. Philip, they claimed, was building up support for himself among the Greeks, even in the Peloponnesos. Ischandros added his personal testimony of Macedonian-subsidized corruption in high Arkadian places. It is not difficult to imagine the sort of argument the *demos* was prepared to accept and act upon: peace with Philip was all very well if that was the only way they could protect themselves against his entry into central Greece, but if the Greek states could be induced to deny him entry, then so much the better. If the Athenians suspected Philip of talking peace while he plotted war, they were not averse to repaying him in the same coin. Although no evidence survives, it is unlikely that Demosthenes publicly opposed this scheme. He had decided that peace with Philip was both expedient and unavoidable, but no doubt was obliged to act circumspectly so as to avoid misunderstanding. But he had no hopes of Euboulos' success and is unlikely to have been enthusiastic.[51]

Among those commissioned was Aischines himself, who was sent to the Peloponnesos; unfortunately the Arkadian reaction to his visit is the only one on which information happens to survive. But it is clear from his report on his return that he had achieved little, if anything; for all his enthusiasm, all he could propose was that further envoys should be sent to denounce the pro-Macedonians. In general, the decree had merely served to show Philip where his difficulties lay.

PLANS FOR A SETTLEMENT

At this point it becomes important to determine what Philip did intend to achieve through the friendship and peace he claimed to want with the Athenians. As we have seen, pressure will already have been exerted upon him at the least to lend assistance to those with an interest in challenging the Persian King's dominion over Asia Minor. At about the time that this subject must have been broached he had in any case been forced to look beyond his Chalkidian alignment and had turned towards rapprochement with Athens. But there was more. First, Macedonia was vulnerable by land rather than by sea; Demosthenes might proclaim the desirability of assigning the Athenian fleet to raids on the Macedonian coasts, patrols along her shoreline and blockades of her harbours,[52] but he probably misled few of those who heard him. However, what did constitute a most serious threat to Macedonia was the possibility of a combination of both Athens and Thebes.[53] In the negotiations which now follow, and in the Peace of Philokrates itself, this is clearly the foremost factor. The second, of lesser importance in the long term, was the question of the role Thrace was to play in the settlement. To put it in Athenian terms: was Athens to be compelled to surrender her own gains in the area, especially those with Kersebleptes, or was she to be obliged – with neither bases nor (except through alliance with Philip himself) allies – to pursue her economic and strategic interests only by the grace and with the permission of the Macedonian king? That both of these factors were clearly recognized in Athens and Pella soon became obvious.

For Philip the climactic point in his dealing with his existing allies and in his longer term intentions regarding the Greek states and (by now) Asia Minor was fast approaching. Whether or not he wished it, he could not avoid intervening in central Greece; his Thessalian alliance depended on it. But to finish off the Phokians' resistance and to deprive them of the will and the ability to resist Boiotian domination in central Greece was to restore Thebes to a level of power from which she had declined only through their efforts and to drive Athens into peace and alliance with her – the combination he had most to avoid. The action he was to take, therefore, whatever fate the Phokians were to suffer, must leave Thebes too weak to damage him. This might come as a surprise to his ally and hers, the Thessalian *koinon*, but he could confidently expect to make the prospect appealing to a Thessaly which would be, as a result, dominant in the Amphiktyonic League. The Athenians, too, ought to find it attractive: their border-town Oropos would be returned to them and Thebes would no longer stand in the way of their influence in Euboia.

The supreme difficulty confronting this plan was that for the moment Thebes was and must remain his ally at least until alliance with Athens instead was assured. So that negotiations with the latter (and probably with Phokis) would have to be carried out without arousing Theban suspicions to a critical level. Provided that there remained no other safeguard open to the Athenians, the king knew by now that they would agree to peace; he knew too that, if he were to insist that he would not have peace without alliance, then they would agree to peace and alliance. The terms, combined with his holding of the Athenian prisoners from Olynthos, should give him the lever he might need to bring Athenian hoplites into play, if necessary, when the Thebans saw what was happening. It was inevitable, that is, that during the coming negotiations Philip would need to emphasize heavily the advantages accruing to Athens from his planned finesse – but without being publicly specific as to how they were to be attained.

The embassies commissioned under the decree of Euboulos, then, represented a setback to his plans – not because they were likely to raise a serious coalition against Macedon in the Peloponnesos or elsewhere, but rather because they indicated that the Athenians were not yet fully convinced that peace with Philip was expedient. In fact, some sixteen months would elapse between their enthusiastic approval for Philokrates' motion and their eventual decision (on the proposal of the same man) to despatch an embassy to learn Philip's terms.

CENTRAL GREECE: THE FIRST INTERVENTION

Since 351 the level of activity in the Sacred War had subsided almost to nothing. The Phokian will to fight seems to have been broken and Thebes was content to let sleeping dogs lie. The meetings of the rebel Amphiktyony had ceased and the leading Phokian allies, Athens and Sparta, had lost interest in a state that no longer offered them a weapon against Thebes. Phalaikos, no longer bothering to maintain the Phokian role of wronged innocence (and, besides, needing the money), cynically plundered the Delphic treasuries. During the spring or early summer of 347, after a series of skirmishes with Boiotian forces, he was removed from office, charged with embezzlement of sacred funds and replaced by a triumvirate of commanders, Deinokrates, Kallias and Sophanes. In the ensuing investigations the blame fell upon his administrator of sacred properties, one Philon.[54] From their three fortresses in Boiotia, Orchomenos, Koroneia and Korsiai,[55] the new leaders engaged upon so successful a campaign that, its territory ravaged, and unable to withstand the Phokian mercenary forces, the Boiotian League appealed to Philip.

For him the situation was difficult. While, no doubt, he would be better able to find support for his plans in the disgruntled Phalaikos, and consequently welcomed his demotion, he had also to keep some sort of faith with his Theban ally. On the other hand, he could hardly intervene definitively in central Greece until he had alliance with Athens. His sole alternative, therefore, was to commit only a few troops in answer to the appeal, enough to avoid losing his allies, but not enough to finish the war before he was ready to end it on his own terms. He was, as Diodoros says, delighted at the Theban plight and disposed to see them humiliated. But for the moment they must be kept guessing.[56] The leader of the Macedonian force was probably Parmenion (Antipatros being, at this time or shortly afterwards, in Thrace), who was a few months later (perhaps on his return from Boiotia) to lead the siege of Halos which was in progress by the end of the following winter.

The Phokians were currently attempting to establish a fortress near Abai, a town on the Phokian border opposite Orchomenos and Tegyra. Attacking the enemy there, the Boiotians, with their Macedonian support, won a victory but made no attempt to go farther.[57]

ATHENIAN COUNTER-MEASURES

So half-hearted an intervention may not in itself have impressed a sense of urgency upon the anti-Macedonians of Athens; but what it presaged clearly did. They could no longer doubt that the Thebans would call for larger efforts by Philip and would, if necessary, assist in his passage through Thermopylai. It was only a matter of time. As Aischines later said, it was by now, when the envoys despatched by the decree of Euboulos half a year or more ago had returned without a shadow of support, that he and others like him began thinking in terms of peace.[58] But, first, steps must be taken quickly to ensure that Athens was able to bargain from strength. Demosthenes too, who procured for himself membership of the Boulē at about this time,[59] perceived the urgency of the situation and spoke of a plan 'to protect the islanders and the Hellespontine cities'. Philip, these people saw, would wish to complete the eradication of Athenian influence in Thrace before the terms of peace could restrain him. Resolutions were moved by Euboulos, Aristophon and Diopeithes and a force was sent out, probably under Chares, to the Chersonesos. Here contact was made with Kersebleptes and the combined forces established a number of garrisons along the Propontid and Aegean coasts.[60] Myrtenon was fortified, and Doriskos, just to the west of the Hebros mouth (in Amadokos' territory), as also were Ergiske and Serrion, the latter a promontory near Doriskos. On the Propontis, Ganos was taken and nearby Hieron Oros. It is not clear whether any Athenian soldiers were left to man these outposts; on the whole it is more likely that their ally Kersebleptes maintained them.[61]

This was a disquieting setback to the progress of Philip's peace-negotiations. The garrisons themselves evidently presented no serious military problem (they were quickly and easily overturned six or eight months later), and for the moment he was content to order Antipatros into the area of Hieron Oros with orders to secure a base for later operations.[62] More worrying was the prospect that any Athenian gains would inevitably delay – even prevent – the opening of negotiations.

Encouraged by this success the Athenians turned to Thermopylai, whence Philip must come. If he were to be stopped then this would be only with Phokian help. In very late 347, the new Phokian commanders, chastened by the recent first appearance of Macedonian troops in central Greece, began to cast about for assistance and, in particular, for a means of inducing the Athenians and Spartans to abandon their movement towards the Macedonian camp. To both cities they sent envoys, offering to hand over the strategic towns of Alponos, Thronion and Nikaia, which commanded the central Greek approaches to Thermopylai. Both allies accepted. The Athenians decreed that these towns be taken over by the general Proxenos, that 50 triremes should be launched and that all able-bodied men up to the age of 40 should serve in the expedition.[63] In the southern Thessalian perioecic state of Phthiotis, trouble was flaring which might also be exploited to Philip's disadvantage. Halos, a pro-Athenian coastal town at the southern edge of the Krokion Plain (Crocus Field) and on the main route south from Larisa, Pherai and Pagasai, was at loggerheads with Pharsalos, some 40–50 kilometres to the northwest. Since Halos could be supplied and relieved from the sea, the Athenians could assist in its cause.[64] The Thracian campaign had been a success and the Halian resistance was at the least a useful diversion; all that remained was to take possession of the Pass of Thermopylai. At the end of 347, then, the Athenian position looked strong; and if negotiations could be delayed a little longer the peace might even prove dispensable.

Therefore, probably in December 347 or January 346, a new decree was passed despatching envoys to all the Hellenes to invite them to Athens.[65] This was significantly different from the decree of Euboulos more than a year before, in that the earlier decision had represented the attempt of the Athenians to organize a large-scale effort to meet Philip's advance with military strength, whereas the present measure was an invitation to deliberate on war, if that were necessary, or on peace if that were considered the better course.[66] This more realistic effort clearly belongs in the context of recent Athenian successes. The first steps had been taken towards a massive show of resistance to Philip. If enough other states were interested this might be proceeded with; otherwise they might all share in the peace, the terms of which would consequently be much less favourable to Philip.

STAMPEDE FOR PEACE

By mid winter, Philip's plans for his central Greek intervention were in severe jeopardy. He would need to erase the new Athenian advantage in coastal Thrace, but, more pressingly, he could secure his path to Thermopylai only by taking up the Pharsalian cause. Accordingly he ordered Parmenion (whose small command in Boiotia may recently have ended) to invest Halos and bring it to heel. At the same time he might test the Phokian wind to see whether he could forestall Athenian expectations there. Envoys were sent in secret to treat with Phalaikos and probably to persuade other influential Phokians (and perhaps, by attractive bribes, their mercenaries) to support the reinstatement of their demoted commander.[67]

Tension was high among the Athenians, for whom precise timing was now as important as it was for Philip. There had been no rejection of Philip's peace-offers, but as yet they had been unprepared to take the actual decision to negotiate. Once they and their allies took possession of Thermopylai and once the other Greek states indicated their support either for war or for an Athenian-dominated peace, then would be the time to act. Probably for some time now representations had been made, at least by the families concerned, for the release by Philip of the Athenians he had taken prisoner at Olynthos. In addition, if their release could be effected before peace-negotiations began, a powerful Macedonian advantage would be removed. By the beginning of winter the matter had been taken up officially by Philokrates and Demosthenes, with the result that Aristodemos, a friend of the king and member of the acting profession (whose itinerant and somewhat privileged existence made it suitable for such missions),[68] was instructed to sound out Philip on the question of the prisoners' release and to report to the *demos*. On his return to Athens there was a delay. He was not summoned to the Boulē to make his report. On the flimsiest of excuses – his alleged preoccupation with private business – so important a matter was temporarily suppressed.[69] Philip, seeing that the Athenian *demos* might be made to work on his behalf against its own leaders, took the initiative of releasing one prisoner, Iatrokles, who returned home in late Gamelion or at the beginning of Anthesterion (late January or early February) to report that Philip wanted peace.

Events quickly followed the course for which Philip had hoped. Angry at having been denied Aristodemos' report, many people pressed for his summons before the Boulē. On the demand of Demokrates of Aphidna the order was given and the envoy appeared, conveying Philip's great friendship towards the city and adding (for the first time, to our knowledge, that this was made explicit) that the king was eager not only for peace but also for alliance. At the assembly at which these tidings were reported, in the first days of Anthesterion, a second bombshell shattered the expectations of those who hoped that the new Athenian initiatives could reduce or erase Philip's bargaining strength. Shortly after the Phokian triumvirate's offer of Thermopylai, it had become known that Phalaikos had returned to the Phokian command. Proxenos had been sent to him to discover whether the agreement with his predecessors still stood, but he had been utterly rebuffed. His letter containing this information, as well as a report by the sacred heralds that the Phokians had refused to accept the truce for the Lesser Mysteries, were both received by this same meeting of the Assembly.[70] The timing was masterly. The *demos*, now eager for peace, was jubilant, and the most powerful ammunition of those who counselled delay was destroyed. Demosthenes, with the horse gone, wasted no time in trying to bolt the stable door; he stood and proposed a motion to confer a crown on Aristodemos for his efforts. It would thereafter be difficult, because of this promptitude, to accuse him of any connection with the delay – although his motion (as he perhaps did not foresee or was prepared to rationalize at another time) was to prove a source of embarrassment in the days after the *demos* turned against the peace.[71]

No further delay was possible. Philokrates, realizing that speed was now of the essence, that the earlier agreement could be reached, the sooner the present Thracian possessions of each side might be guaranteed them by its terms, moved the immediate establishment of an embassy of ten to learn Philip's conditions.[72] The Macedonian manoeuvres were thus successful. The Athenians were galloping headlong down the road to peace, out of the control of their leaders, who could do little but attempt to preserve what little initiative was left to them.

The effect on the uncommitted states may be imagined. More than two months later, by mid-Elaphebolion, no Greek states had responded to the Athenian invitation to discuss war or peace. Whether or not the Hellenes might have reacted differently had the Athenians not taken unilateral action in the meantime we cannot tell. But, whatever the result might have been, no envoys would ever come now.[73] Philip knew he had won the first round – provided, at least, that he could re-take coastal Thrace and subordinate Kersebleptes. The second round – to persuade the Athenian to join him in an assault on Theban power – had yet to be fought.

THE FIRST EMBASSY

The envoys left Attica by sea, probably from the region of Marathon or Rhamnous on the northwestern coast, crossed to Euboia, to avoid Boiotia, and travelled north to Oreos at its northern tip. A herald with authority to escort them thence to Pella had not yet arrived so, rather than delay, they crossed without him to Halos, still under siege but open by sea to the Athenian fleet. After making contact with Parmenion, who no doubt provided them with some form of safe conduct, they lost no time in pushing northwards across the Krokion Plain and through Pagasai and Pherai to Larisa, where the official escort met them for the remaining 150 km. to Pella. The journey will have taken them perhaps a week.[74]

Around the middle of Anthesterion (*c.* 12 March) this first Athenian embassy arrived in Pella 'to discuss with Philip the matter of peace and the common interests of the Athenians and Philip'.[75] Summoned to an audience with the king the envoys delivered one by one, from oldest to youngest, the speeches they had prepared. Undoubtedly the most significant were those of men with the stature of Nausikles (the commander of the Athenian force at Thermopylai in 352) and Philokrates. But nothing is known of their submissions. In the trial of Aischines three years later, without which we should have had no information at all on the matter, a summary of Aischines' speech alone survives. It is no more – if genuine – than a rhetorical display-piece on the subject of Amphipolis, though perhaps appropriate enough in the mouth of the next-to-youngest ambassador (Demosthenes being the most junior), who therefore spoke second-last, when all the important subjects had been exhausted by others.[76] Demosthenes, in the concluding address, was – so Aischines claimed – badly affected by nervousness and was unable to complete his piece.[77]

Aischines' topic will no doubt have appealed to the Athenian audience, who got it second-hand, but few of the more astute will have imagined that Philip accorded it any serious attention. Four subjects however, probably treated by the most senior speakers, must have been taken seriously. Two of them, so events were to show, and as he no doubt rejoindered, were not regarded by the king as negotiable: the independence of the Thracian coastal forts and the matter of the naval assistance Athens was giving to Halos. As regards the latter there was simply nothing to be discussed; whether or not Athenian aid before this point had been official, it will now have been terminated and there is no suggestion among the few references to the subsequent fate of Halos that it was an Athenian military loss. When it was delivered at a second audience, the king's answer to the question of the Thracian forts will have been equally unequivocal. As the envoys could well see, his preparations for a Thracian campaign were complete. He would not tolerate the presence of bases that interfered with the sovereignty of his Byzantian, Perinthian and Thracian allies; nor would he leave unpunished a Thracian ruler who, the ally of Macedon, had turned to peace with the Athenians when they were his enemies and, since that time, had acknowledged Athens' claim to the Macedonian town of Amphipolis and had been guilty of territorial crimes against the allies of Philip.[78]

However, to say this was not to deny that the Athenians were legitimately concerned with the passageway to the Black Sea. Philip would not dispute their claim to the Chersonesos; he promised that he would not take his army there while deliberations were in progress and, in accordance with the terms he was proposing, the peace itself would guarantee its subsequent security, for each party would by right retain the territories it then possessed.[79]

The fourth vital subject must have been the Phokian war. Philip's own intentions for its settlement and his need, in the meantime, to retain his Boiotian allies prevented him from being completely open with the envoys, at least in public, and certainly prohibited his committing anything on the matter to writing. He may have gone so far as to point out that, once it was possible to do so and provided that he had the support of Athens in full alliance, he would view the relative claims of Phokis and Thebes in much the same way as did the Athenians, to judge by their support for the former over the years of the Sacred War; until then, of course, the Phokians must be excluded from the treaty.[80] Above all he will have stressed that he must have alliance as well as peace.[81]

There must have been some discussion on the subject of the Athenian prisoners taken at Olynthos, although this is not specifically attested until the visit of the second embassy.[82] At this stage, no doubt, he pointed out (what he must already have told Aristodemos) that he would consider neither holding nor demanding payment for his own allies; their release was therefore in the Athenians' own hands. He will also have added the several inducements he was reported to have promised (but which, when the alliance neither operated as he had hoped nor showed any signs of permanency, he was unable to realise): Athenian influence would be restored in Euboia; Oropos would be restored to her; the Boiotian towns, Thespiai and Plataia, would be repopulated; and Philip would cut a channel across the narrow neck of the Chersonesos, severing it from the mainland.[83] None of these offers represented any loss to him and all should have been welcome to Athens. The first three would be both instruments and consequences of his planned circumscription of Theban power; but, as such, they would also be dependent on it. The fourth, although it may have removed a minor naval hazard facing the Athenian corn-fleet, was also complementary to his guarantee not to interfere in the Chersonesos; he would render the Athenian territory more easily defensible against assault from the Thracian mainland.

Now Philip well realized how much would depend on the ten men who were to return to their fellows with his terms. He would send back a letter with them pointing out that he was in a position to confer great benefits upon the *demos*, but he must remain vague once it came to details.[84] It would be the envoys themselves who conveyed, at least in general terms, the real import of this alliance.

THE THRACIAN CAMPAIGN OF SPRING 346

As they left Pella, around 20 Anthesterion (= *c.* 18 March), Philip also left, bound for Thrace. Kersebleptes had – until the time of his cooperation with the Athenians in establishing their coastal forts – lain quiet since his defeat by Philip and the latter's Perinthian, Byzantian and central Thracian allies in 351. It may have been that at that time his son had been taken hostage and remained in Pella,[85] which, if so, may provide us with the explanation. In the campaign that now follows, which lasted only three months, there appear to have been only two aims: to defeat Kersebleptes and subordinate him to Macedonian interests and to remove the newly planted bases on the coasts. The first of these objects was achieved in about a month, by 23 Elaphebolion (= *c.* 20 April). Philip pushed eastwards directly to the Propontis, perhaps to a base at Apros secured for him several months before by Antipatros, and there defeated the Thracian forces at the Hieron Oros stronghold. Not until *c.* 23 Thargelion (= *c.* 18 June), however, did he return to Pella,[86] and we must take it that, on completing his arrangements with Kersebleptes, he proceeded to pick off the remaining hostile bases – a task that was in all probability fairly straightforward, since word reaching their defenders (if any remained) must have made it quite clear to them that they would certainly be given no support.[87]

During the Thracian campaign of 352/1, during which he had fought in alliance with, among others, Amadokos of central Thrace, it may be that he had annexed the western Thracian area previously held by the sons of Berisades.[88] But, if not in 351, then certainly in 346, the eastern frontier of Macedonia must have been extended to the Nestos. Of Amadokos, in whose kingdom Doriskos and Serrion (and perhaps Myrtenon and Ergiske) lay, nothing is known after his participation in the campaign five years earlier. He had been by then, it seems, a very old man[89] and was most probably dead by 346. His successor was evidently a certain Teres, who fought, as the inheritor of his Macedonian alliance, alongside Philip.[90] Kersebleptes was not removed from his throne, which he still occupied four years later. But it is likely that he was obliged at the very least to renew his violated alliance with Philip.

Before leaving Pella on this campaign Philip had given orders to three of his most senior commanders, Antipatros, Parmenion and

Eurylochos,[91] to act on his behalf in Athens and, provided its Assembly accepted his terms, to receive the oaths of ratification from the proper magistrates.

THE PEACE OF PHILOKRATES

The Athenian ambassadors arrived home in the last days of Anthesterion, probably by the 27th (= c. 25 March), where they made their reports to the Council and to the Assembly. On the motion of Demosthenes, it was resolved that, when the Macedonian envoys arrived, the mandatory two consecutive days should be set for assembly-meetings. By the time they did arrive – and perhaps they delayed intentionally to just this end – the city Dionysia, which would prevent the transaction of non-festival business for its duration (9–13 Elaphebolion), was too near, and the 18th and 19th were set.[92]

We should recognize the difficult situation in which the Athenian ambassadors found themselves on their return. They, like most of the *demos*, were – now if not before – in favour of a peace;[93] but they alone knew the terms under which Philip was prepared to concede it. From the popular reaction on the first day of debate to Philokrates' motion (which was undoubtedly formulated in the terms Philip had dictated), it is clear, however, that the envoys had not given proper emphasis in their report to some of the conditions on which Philip insisted, notably the exclusion from the treaty of the Phokians, the Halians and Kersebleptes. Again, although we know almost nothing of the role played in the debate by any envoys other than Philokrates, Demosthenes and Aischines, it appears that, at least of these three, only Philokrates exhibited the moral courage to stand by the only terms Philip would accept. This was an unpleasant task that most were evidently prepared to leave to Philokrates and to Philip's own envoys.

When the *demos* assembled on 18 Elaphebolion (= c. 15 April) and other, minor matters had been dealt with,[94] it had before it not one motion but two. The first was Philokrates' in the form of a *probouleuma*, containing the proposal of peace and alliance on Philip's terms, a treaty open to Philip and his allies on the one side and Athens and the remnants of her naval league on the other, and with the specific exclusions already noted. Both parties were to retain what possessions they had at the date of ratification.[95] The *demos*, taken by surprise, reacted strongly against the motion, supporting overwhelmingly the alternative proposal, a *dogma* of their allied synod which recommended that no decision should be taken in the absence of the Athenian embassies to the Hellenes, but that on their return the question of peace (without alliance) again be debated. This was a proposal for Common Peace, in which all Greeks would be free to take part, if they so desired, at any time within three months of its establishment.[96]

All speakers (who certainly included Aischines and Demosthenes but not, presumably, Philokrates) gave support to the allied motion[97] – and, in so doing, these men who knew Philip's intentions were at best hypocritical. Since debate on the peace had been confined by Demosthenes' earlier procedural motion to the first day, allowing on the 19th only the actual vote, it was clear that the *demos* was unwittingly pursuing a line that would destroy all hope of peace. Demosthenes with his own procedural motion in mind, moved that the Macedonian envoys be summoned before the assembly, ready – now that his own (false) stance had been sufficiently demonstrated – to fasten on Philip himself the responsibility for Philokrates' peace. Aischines, apparently feeling that it would be better to leave this to the following day, when the procedural block on further debate could be rescinded, successfully adjourned discussion until the morning.[98]

On the morning of the 19th, Demosthenes rose and – no doubt still professing support for the allied motion – announced that the previous day's discussion was worthless unless Philip would agree to its terms. Calling Antipatros to the platform, he put to him the question whether the king would accept Common Peace without alliance. As the envoys all knew, he would not.[99] Thus, when the prohibition against further debate had been lifted,[100] discussion was resumed. If Demosthenes spoke at all – which seems unlikely – it cannot have been in favour of Philokrates' *probouleuma*.[101] The task of winning over the *demos* was left to others, Aischines, Euboulos and Kephisophon, against opposition from Aristophon and others.[102] Perhaps what swung the balance in the end was the blunt warning of Euboulos: either Athens must mobilize immediately for war and make the requisite arrangements to pay for it; or she must accept Philokrates' (Philip's) peace. The motion was carried, but not without amendment, for the clause excluding Phokis, Halos and Kersebleptes was struck from the text.[103] Demosthenes, like the others, knew this would be unacceptable to Philip, but decided that it was a fault that could be remedied later.

When the assembly dissolved, the Boulē met and set a date (the 24th) for another special meeting of the people at which a decision was to be made on the question how the Athenians' allies were to give their oaths to Philip. In preparation for this meeting both Demosthenes and Philokrates moved a *probouleuma* that 'the synod-representatives of the allies this day give their oaths to the envoys from Philip';[104] the synod contained no representatives of Phokis, Halos or Kersebleptes. On the